BOOKS BY CAROL EISEN RINZLER

Your Adolescent: An Owner's Manual 1981
The Girl Who Got All the Breaks 1980

AS CAROL G. EISEN

Nobody Said You Had to Eat off the Floor 1971

Introduction

From *Webster's New International Dictionary*, Second Edition, published in 1947:

> adolescence: 1. The state or process of growing up from childhood to manhood or womanhood; youth or the period of life between puberty and maturity extending in legal use to the attainment of full legal age or majority; specif. Educa., the period of life extending from the end of a person's elementary course to the end of his high school course. 2. Physical geography. Topographic adolescence.

From *Webster's New International Dictionary*, Third Edition, published in 1961:

> adolescence: 1. The state or process of growing up; the period of life from puberty to maturity terminating legally at the age of majority. 2. The transition from youth to maturity in the cycle of stream erosion, valley development, or regional sculpture by running water.

If you are given, as I am, to pondering, you easily can while away a pleasant half-hour pondering how the changing definition of a simple word reflects our changing society. Was the writer of the Third someone, perhaps the parent of an adolescent, who, with a throwing up of the hands at the idea of anything being defined by schooling any longer, had taken to the woods?

In any case, I should define my own terms. Adolescence, for

the purposes of this book, begins the first time your previously worshipful child looks at you the way you looked at your own mother or father when she or he said no to lipstick or tackle. As for when adolescence ends, I considered an age cut-off, but then I thought that one adolescent's fifteen was another adolescent's eighteen and another's thirty-two.[1] For the purposes of this book, then, adolescence ends when your child drives off by itself in a car, thenceforth to do Terrible Things Over Which You Have No Control.

I did do some research, outside the privacy of my own home, for this book. I read a lot of magazines that made me a hit at parties. ("Is it Farrah and Ryan or Farrah and Burt, or Ryan and Burt, do you suppose?" beats supply-side economics as an ice-breaker any day.) I spoke to a lot of my friends, and I interviewed adolescents older and/or more swinging than my own, who later told their own parents they were afraid they had corrupted me. I am indebted to Carolyn Anthony, Joni Evans, Lois, Bob, Tony, and Roger Gould, Judith Kern, Phyllis and Dick Kluger, Alice Kosner, Stephanie and Judith Richter, Merri Rosenberg, Gail and Maura Sheehy, Jill, Erica, and Paul Spelman, and Naomi Warner.[2]

[1] For some, of course, the cut-off is never. Consider how touched you are when a friend telephones to assure himself that you have arrived home safely. Now consider how you feel when a parent calls for the same reason. "I'm lying out in the middle of the highway bleeding to death," you snap. Whenever I dine at a restaurant with my father, a distinguished gentleman in full command of his faculties, I check to make sure he has left a tip.

[2] Also to Susan Boynton, Tracy Klein, Page Lichtenfeld, Susanna Loeb, Jono Mermin, Clare Ramsey, and Nancy Samson, friends of my children who originally were integrated above but who were distinguished at my children's suggestion, and to whom I am in theory no longer indebted since they are now immortal.

But for all that research, there still is not much in this book about drugs, promiscuity, or depression. When I was in college my English professor said one should write about what one knows, and thus far I am fortunate in knowing very little about those things. My own adolescents, I am profoundly grateful to say, have spared me. (I thought long and hard about the reasons for that and concluded it was primarily dumb luck.)

Another reason there is not much in this book about drugs, promiscuity, or depression is that there is nothing funny about those subjects. And I did want to write a funny book. If we can accompany our children through adolescence with a little more laughter and a little less anger and grief, we may be able to keep some of those terrible things ever from happening.

YOUR ADOLESCENT:
AN OWNER'S MANUAL

Selecting the Model That's Right for You

If you have enjoyed owning a small child, now is the time to move up to an adolescent. The American Way presents its 1980s models, one of which is sure to meet your needs and fit your budget.

The Basic Adolescent

The standard model, suitable for everyday use, comes with its own telephone receiver permanently attached. Food costs are nominal, even on the male version, provided you own a cow. For the budget-conscious, two super-economy specials: with down upholstery omitted (available only in tropical climates); without record and tape attachments (available only in areas without electricity).

The Basic Adolescent Plus Hair

The most popular of the option-added models, the Plus Hair costs only a few thousand dollars more a year to operate. Arrives equipped with a twenty-year supply of shampoo and conditioner and its own color-coordinated blow dryer. Male model actually makes its own appointments with barber. Female model's accessories include: hot rollers, clips, hairspray, curling iron, end papers, rinse, ribbons, and a generous selection of $10 barrettes. A good investment for parents who plan to open a drugstore someday.

The All-American

A perennial best-seller. Guaranteed not to drop out of school. Standard equipment includes panel component system with direct radiating tweeter, two desirable extra-curricular activities, orthodontic braces, and summer camp. Strong powers of concentration (can sit through the same movie seven times), memory (knows who ate lunch with whom three months ago), and analytic skills (can distinguish among Styx, Led Zeppelin, the Clash, Black Sabbath, and Martha and the Muffins).

The Royal

When only the best will do. Includes all features of the All-American plus: upholstered in designer jeans and co-ordinated T-shirts with imprints not offensive to grandparents, color TV. Reads and writes English. Your choice of varsity letter, class political office, honor roll, or never sits home on Saturday nights. Optional extras include: private bath, private telephone, private school, something to do on long private-school vacations.

The Classic

Available once again after a twenty-year absence. Incompatible with drug, alcohol, and premarital-sex attachments. Wants to be admitted to an Ivy League college and is guaranteed to produce at least one (legitimate) grandchild. Sends thank-you notes and knows proper use of the subjunctive. Experimental model sports classic vocabulary (e.g., "You won't respect me"), and rises when adult enters room.

BASIC
MODEL
U.S.
MAIL

Filling It Up

Women who run corporations and hold doctorates in nuclear engineering, even women resourceful, intelligent, and motivated enough to find an honest garage mechanic, realize they have met their match when it comes to getting small children to eat. I remember one six-month period during my son's toddlership when he ingested nothing but Libby's Vienna sausages and apple juice, a circumstance that bothered neither the pediatrician nor me overmuch, although it was embarrassing when my husband's parents visited. Occasionally this problem persists into adolescence, especially among dating female adolescents, who feel that if you want to see a picture of someone with a really great figure, you should look at one of those ads that start, "Only sixteen dollars a month will feed little Mei Lin and her family of eight."

Most adolescents, however, increase their food intake and with it their range. The dill pickle no longer represents the outermost limit of culinary experimentation; there is the euphoria of laying aside your copy of *Chopmeat Cavalcade* and settling in to cook for a person who no longer insists that a sandwich is inedible because it has been cut diagonally instead of horizontally, or that fresh orange juice is undrinkable because of the "floaties" and "sinkies." (Broken cookies still taste yucky, but any adult can tell you that.) Culinary adventurousness is particularly pronounced in adolescents who have younger siblings, since this permits the adolescent (a) to show its superiority ("Jane, you're so stupid. You won't eat anything but hamburger") and (b) to

improvise new and imaginative forms of torture ("Hey, Mom, why don't you make squid? I bet I'd love squid. You'd love squid, too, Jane, if you weren't so stupid").

Except for keeping a supply of bologna and white rice around for younger siblings, then, menu-planning for your adolescent is not much of a problem. Except, of course, for breakfast, a grossly boring meal and one that is served at an hour (the middle of the night) when no normal person is hungry and no sentient human being should be forced into the company of those who smile or speak pleasantly. (An adolescent who is cheerful at breakfast should be kept home from school that day.) Weekend (post-noon) breakfasts, on the other hand, allow your adolescent to display all the creativity of its newly awakened taste buds by conceiving truly disgusting food combinations. Often these are in the form of an omelet. "Boy, what I'd really like this morning is a guacamole omelet," says your adolescent cheerfully. "Boy, I'd really enjoy that." "I'm sorry," you say, crushed. "I don't think we have any avocadoes. How about an artichoke-heart omelet? We have artichoke hearts," you say and reel off in the cadences of a late-night television commercial for things-that-julienne a list of omelet possibilities that rivals Madame Romaine's. "No," says your adolescent sadly, "I just won't have anything."

Adventurousness has bounds, notably liver, all fish except tuna, egg salad, and anything that comes from an animal your adolescent once saw a movie about (bunny rabbits, duckies, Bambi). Dinner out now means more than choosing between McDonald's and Burger King but rarely extends to French food. This may be because your adolescent can't always be sure what's in or under those sauces, or it may be that some time ago an adolescent in Manhattan, taken to a French restaurant by its grandparents, ordered something that sounded promising and wound up with calves' brains on its plate.[1] French restaurants also are not noted for swiftness of service, and while your adolescent is willing to eat more eclectically, it is not necessarily eager to spend much more time in the process. Your adolescent has better things to do with its time than to eat; eating, therefore, is better done while also doing something else, like reading, or talking on the phone, or attending classes, or using the fact that you were too well brought up to make scenes in restaurants with tablecloths to choose dinner out with you as the right time to announce it has decided to dye its hair green.

Difficult to please are adolescents with special dietary re-

[1] Occasionally, however, you will hit a genuine gourmet, an adolescent who eats Tiptree Little Scarlet strawberry jam with its thumb and forefinger and on tasting a wedge of nine-dollar-a-pound Bucheron cheese says, "Hey, that's pretty good," leaving you shortly thereafter with only Cheez Whiz to serve to your guests.

quirements who also have a line in to *The New England Journal of Medicine.* Typically, after you have detoxified the entire house, erasing even the memory of a Hershey Bar ("I'll eat it if it's here"), the adolescent announces that new studies prove chocolate is harmless but there is no way it can eat the shrimp you are serving for dinner. Shellfish, new studies prove, is death, and the instant coffee in the vanilla mousse will stunt its growth. In fact, it might as well just run down to McDonald's for a burger, fries, and shake because, new studies prove, the thing about fried food is a myth.[2]

[2]MOTHER RINZLER'S VICIOUSLY HOSTILE CHOCOLATE CAKE

Butter and flour a 9 x 13 pan.

Preheat oven to 350°.

In your food processor fitted with the plastic blade (recipe also can be made without food processor, but you will not stay angry long enough to cream the butter) cream well together:

½ cup butter
1 cup sugar

Add, one at a time, beating well after each:

4 eggs

Now add and blend:

1 tsp. vanilla
1 16-ounce can chocolate syrup

Blend in, using a brief on-and-off motion, for just a few seconds:

1 cup self-rising flour

Now remove the top of the food processor and mix in with your rubber spatula:

1 12-ounce package semi-sweet chocolate chips

Bake at 350° for 45 to 50 minutes. Cool and then sprinkle with confectioner's sugar before serving.

Also difficult to please is the adolescent whose tastes have become so educated they have left your own tastebuds hopelessly behind, still picking their way through nouvelle cuisine. The same person who would not swallow a vitamin pill unless it was shaped like a tiny cave person now has commandeered an entire cabinet for foods you had thought were eaten only by fish. One mother was distraught because her daughter appeared to be surviving on a diet of unhulled sesame seeds (for calcium) and yeast flakes (for energy), while greeting all ordinary food with the comment, "Are you trying to poison me?" The mother arrived home one day to find her adolescent dipping with oddly metronomic regularity into a large bowl of fruit. "What are you doing?" asked the mother. "I'm on a grape fast," announced the daughter. "You eat one grape every seven seconds. You can eat a hundred pounds of grapes in a day and still lose weight." The mother felt much better after she had a nice cup of caffeine-rich black coffee and a Twinkie.

Study Skills

Is This Your Adolescent's Study Schedule?

4:00 P.M. Adolescent arrives home from school. If mother is home, adolescent asks why she hasn't gotten a job yet or gone back to med school or otherwise done something productive with her life. If mother is at work, adolescent makes note to self to discuss at dinner high incidence of drug use among children of working mothers.

4:01–4:10 If boy: Opens refrigerator and cabinets, eats onion dip, Doritos, 3 Mallomars, 2 glasses milk. Tells or leaves note for mother nothing in house to eat.

If girl: As above, except eats 1 container boysenberry yoghurt, 1 ounce kelp, 2 Mallomars. Leaves note for or tells mother nothing in house to eat except disgusting fattening food.

4:11–4:15 Enters room, finds desk, turns on radio.

4:16 Opens Chemistry book.

4:17 Decides cannot understand homework and requires consultation with Chemistry authority. Calls best friend.

4:18–4:29 Discusses who Chemistry teacher picked on today, whether Jimmy's T-shirt really meant what it said, whether a microprocessor-controlled quartz synthesizer for its tuner would give life meaning.

4:30–4:35 Victimizes younger sibling.

4:36–4:40 Studies Chemistry.

4:41–4:59 Studies face in mirror. Discovers three new pimples.

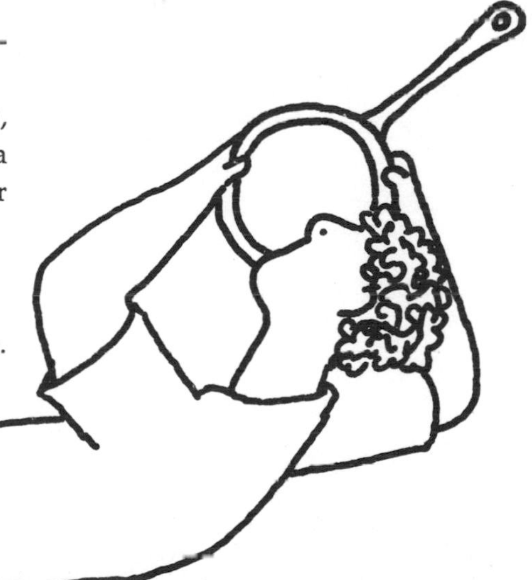

Searches Chemistry book for information on undetectable and painless poisons. Drafts suicide note. Notices one eyebrow distinctly hairier than other. Wonders why friends have never commented on deformity. Tries to remember what it has heard about cancer of the eyebrow, especially whether it is so instantly fatal there is no point in doing Chemistry homework.

5:00–5:05 Takes phone call from desirable person of opposite sex who asks questions about Chemistry homework.

5:06–5:25 Telephones best friend. Discusses whether prior telephone caller really wanted to discuss Chemistry homework or had something else on mind. Discusses when to make plans to discuss plans for what to do this weekend.

5:26–5:32 Studies Chemistry.

5:33–5:35 Wonders whether grades would improve if switched from looseleaf notebook to spiral-bounds.

5:36–5:48 Takes telephone survey of friends about correlation between spiral-bound notebooks and grades.

5:49–6:15 Goes out and buys spiral-bound notebook.

6:16–6:30 Eats dinner. Asks to be excused after main course because too much homework to do.

6:31–6:40 Listens to music to get back in mood to study.

6:41–6:55 Puts new tabs on new notebook dividers.

6:56–7:00 Studies Chemistry. . . .

If this is the situation in your house, you need help in forming better study habits. Try the following:

How to Do Your Homework

1. Be willing to work. Your grade-school child's assignments may rarely have challenged you, especially if you were smart. Now, though, you'll be thrown in with a whole new group of parents, some of whom may be better prepared for high school than you, and the assignments will be on a level meant to get you ready for your offspring's college work. Don't let this throw you, though. If you're willing to put in the time and pay close attention, you'll do fine!

2. Make sure you know what the assignment is. It's true that adolescents sometimes are not completely clear when they hand out assignments. But more often, parents are careless listeners. It's your responsibility to know what your adolescent wants you to do. Before you start a homework assignment, make sure you understand exactly what's required; read the directions. Otherwise, you will make unnecessary work for yourself and find yourself still awake at two in the morning conjugating Latin verbs in the past pluperfect because you wasted all that time on the perfective future.

3. Learn to type. It's sensible to make this investment in your adolescent's high-school career, and you really will need the skill when you get it to college. Teachers like assignments they can read. Added bonus! You won't have to spend extra hours forging your adolescent's handwriting. What about shorthand? Probably not necessary unless your adolescent takes voluminous class notes and needs you to transcribe them.

4. Develop good study habits. Start doing your homework as soon as your adolescent arrives home from school. If you have a job, of course, your homework will have to wait a bit, but if you're organized, you can do some of it while you're preparing dinner. Have a neat, well-lighted area where you can work, and keep yourself free of distractions, like listening to Mozart or worrying about the brief that's due tomorrow.

5. Don't leave things until the last minute. Nobody likes to be up all night typing a paper, and as the parent of an adolescent, with all your new responsibilities, you need your rest! Get started as soon as work is assigned, and allow plenty of time. That may mean curtailing your social life, especially on school nights, but you certainly don't want to be like the parents who came home at midnight to find on the hall table a four-page theme with a note that read, "Please get all topic sentences at beginning of paragraph."

6. Don't be afraid to ask for help. Nothing can make a parent feel worse than to be handed an assignment he or she can't make head or tail of. Unless your adolescent expressly has forbidden you to do so, use sources that will help you understand and do your homework better. Your friends who majored in History or English can be very useful at paper-writing time, provided they aren't too busy with their own adolescents' homework. Hint for single parents: Why not choose a new spouse on the basis of his or her areas of expertise? Imagine the security of knowing that there's someone in the house who can take over on, say, the Physics and German.

7. Don't feel bad if your grades aren't good at first. High school is a lot different from elementary school. It's not as easy to get high marks. Sometimes a mother who, say, receives only a B-plus on her high school freshman's English theme feels disappointed and confused, especially if she is a professional writer who earns three-thousand dollars an article. Cheer up! Other parents are going through the same thing you are. Settle in, sharpen those pencils, and promise yourself you'll work a little harder. Not only will that pull up your grades, but it will help you to feel confident when it's time to write your child's college application essays.

ATLAS

Is There, Perhaps, Hope?

"The school system in the tiny community of Liberty has received a grant of $16,000 from Oklahoma's Department of Education, under the state's Local Educational Improvement Act (Title IV-C), which enables it to offer students a course on proper manners."

Reported in *Seventeen*,
October, 1980

"The Grateful Dead were scheduled to play a concert in Portland, Oregon. At three o'clock on the morning before the rock concert, a dozen Reed College students went down to the auditorium to make sure they would be able to secure tickets for the legendary band's show. Seven hours later, when the auditorium doors opened, they were still the only ones in line."

Reported in *Esquire*,
October, 1980

No, Probably Not

"*Harvard Crimson* editors found themselves threatened by a lawsuit after they doctored a photograph for the campus newspaper. Discovering that they didn't have an illustration to go with an article on prison conditions, they took a photo of two black Harvard seniors, superimposed a few prison bars, and ran it with their story. The students in the photograph were disturbed and threatened to file suit. . . . To keep the matter out of court, the *Crimson* ran an apology and agreed to a list of compensatory demands from campus minority groups. As part of the agreement the *Crimson* agreed to run the word 'black' with an upper case B. They continued to style the word 'white' with a lower case w."

Reported in *Esquire,*
October, 1980

Investing in America's Future

It is a mistake to conclude that adolescents do not appreciate the value of money. The adolescent's profound respect for money dates back to the first time it no longer could pass for eleven at a movie theater. Its only problem with money is in persuading its parents of the necessity for and ease with which their child can be raised in the style of Princess Caroline of Monaco or a Saudi Arabian princeling.

As usual, the adolescent's first appeal is to reason. If the family stopped frittering away money on fresh vegetables, the adolescent points out, it could afford a pair of hand-tooled western boots; if the family denied itself the frivolity of dental care, the adolescent could get started on its numbered Swiss bank account. When reason fails, the adolescent switches tactics, manipulating its parents into investing in America's future: their child.

The Doctors-Were-Selling-Apples-on-the-Streetcorner Approach

Many children still have the first ten-dollar bill ever tendered by a relative with a hearty "Now spend this on something you really want!" The infant miser's announcement that what he really wanted was to save all his money was rewarded by his thrilled parents with an endless supply of free movie tickets, Wacky Packs, and non-violent comic books. The adolescent miser, who has moved into the hard stuff—frequency synthesized tuners, Krypto wheels, fifty-speed bikes, rock-concert tickets—announces at puberty that it is saving its money to help out with college tuition. It will just Do Without. Properly executed, this maneuver convinces the adolescent's parents that selling the family silver is preferable to suggesting to their child that it touch capital. Thus the parents shell out while the adolescent salts it away.[1]

The Go-Getter Maneuver

Out there with its lemonade stand before the snows have melted, able to turn a Badge-a-Minit concession into a pyramid scheme, the go-getter is exemplified by one seventh-grader whose parents discovered they were paying a baby-sitter to sit in their apartment and watch TV while their daughter was down the hall baby-sitting for a neighbor's pre-schooler.[2]

Unlike the miser, the go-getter has every intention of spending its money, someday. It is always Saving Up. The go-getter so embodies the spirit of What Made America Great that its parents' eyes mist over. "Only sixteen more baby-sitting jobs and I can get those roller skates," says the go-getter gamely. "I bet I'll have them soon enough to catch up with Susie and Jenny who as it happens have already learned to skate backward. On one foot."

The parents of the go-getter, who have begun to view themselves as saviors of the Puritan work ethic, respond by creating employment opportunities at a pay scale for which the Teamsters

[1] If you think it makes a man feel uncomfortable when his wife earns more than he does, you should only know how a mother feels when her adolescent has more in its savings account than she has in hers.
[2] Little is more chilling than to be told by a neighbor, "But she said she needed the money."

would raise Jimmy Hoffa's ghost. At first the parents assign necessary and generally unappetizing tasks that are beyond the scope of the adolescent's normal duties. Fairly quickly, though, the adolescent catches on. The fireplace has been cleaned, the refrigerator defrosted, and all the snow shoveled on the back forty. "Gee," says the parent, "I just can't think of anything that really needs doing around here." "Nothing?" asks the adolescent forlornly. "I just need another two hundred dollars before I can buy my certificate of deposit." Thus it is that thousands of adolescents across the country can be found hanging up their own clothes for five dollars an hour.

The Robin-Hood Caper

Adolescent credit risks rarely prey on their parents, who know a fifteen-year-old deadbeat when they see one. Younger siblings, however, are fair game. "I swear I'll pay it back" is the Robin Hood's motto; the Hood believes in stealing from the rich and giving to itself. "I needed the new Kiss album," explains the Hood when its parent inquires why the younger sibling is crying out in its sleep about rubber hoses. Occasionally an unsuspecting friend or relative falls into the Hood's clutches. "Kevin owes me thirty dollars," complained Kevin's younger sibling to his grandmother. "Well, why don't I give you the thirty dollars and Kevin can owe it to me?" smiled Grandmother. "Hey, great idea," said Kevin.

The Do-Unto-Others Ploy

Along with almost everyone else except nursery-school teachers looking for rainy-day projects, most adolescents feel that it is better to receive than to give. The free spender, however, in appealing to its parent's Better Self, has made a grand intuitive leap. Applauding their child's generosity, the parents pridefully give their adolescent money to buy presents for its friends, who in return buy presents for it. Thus, the free spender perfects the childhood ploy of going with Mommy to the toy store and picking out for a little friend's birthday present something that it likes itself and then accidentally breaking the cellophane wrapping, requiring Mommy to go back to the store to get a fresh one for the friend while the child gets to keep the bad one.

Free spenders are more frequently female than male, primarily because few male adolescents enjoy shopping. Occasionally, however, a male adolescent must buy a gift. Parents are easy—anyone who would repack every Christmas since you were four your Styrofoam ball decorated with corks will be ecstatic if you buy something that comes from a store more exotic than the corner cigar stand. Other relatives are no problem since Mother takes care of shopping for them and always forgets to ask to be reimbursed.

Sometimes, however, the adolescent male must shop for one of its own friends. It cannot entrust its mother with the mission since she (a) might buy something awful unless she has minutely detailed instructions, which she always loses, and (b) may find out whom the present is for. Adolescent boys who must buy presents for adolescent girls divide such girls into two categories: (1) those who like cute things, and (2) those who don't like cute things.[3] Some adolescent girls who don't like cute things do like jewelry, which is okay too, but girls who like neither cute things nor jewelry are treated by adolescent males as adolescent males and receive records. Invariably the record is one the recipient already has or does not have only because it doesn't want it. Most adolescents, however, behave much as gracious adults do, smiling and saying, "Gee, how did you know I wanted

[3] A cute thing is something that causes an adolescent girl to say upon seeing it, "Oh, that's *so* cute!"

this?" or "Hey, great, my old one was full of scratches." Part of the Unwritten Code is that one never demands a thank-you note from a friend.

Adult relatives often will ask you to tell them what your adolescent wants for its birthday or Christmas. This problem has shattered many families, since outside of major appliances it is next to impossible to know what will make your adolescent happy, unless you own an adolescent girl who likes cute things, in which case you are home free so long as you do not mind spending on, say, a candle shaped like an ice-cream soda what you used to spend on a pair of shoes.[4] Parents who, through diligent spying, find out what their adolescent really wants, in a price-range that does not require taking a second mortgage on the house, rarely are willing to divulge that information. In fact, a rarely discussed tragedy of divorce is that two parents no longer can get away with one present.

Never believe your adolescent when it says it doesn't want anything for its birthday because it has everything it wants and people are starving in Cambodia, or when it suggests the family skip Christmas altogether this year because the holiday has become so vulgarly commercial. About twelve hours before the deadline, when you have asked your adolescent for the thirtieth time if it's really sure it doesn't want anything, it will utter the denial with a catch in its throat. That will leave you with time enough only to write a check, for 40 per cent more than you planned to spend, increased by the guilt you feel about not having shopped. Money, your adolescent feels, is the only sort of present for which your taste can be trusted.

[4] Have you noticed that the papers never run those charts any more about how the average Russian has to work three weeks for a pair of shoes?

Take Two, They're Small

Not every adolescent is saving up to hire a Mafia hitperson who will button its younger sibling into cement pajamas prior to a nice dip in the river. Many adolescents have a relatively humane attitude; they feel toward their siblings the way you feel toward, say, your electric yoghurt-maker: It is unnecessary, it takes up space, it sits there and wastes; it would be inappropriate for an electric yoghurt-maker to initiate a conversation.

A significant number of adolescents, however, would prefer that their younger siblings be unplugged permanently. Not that your adolescent contemplates violence. Even if murder was its original impulse at an age when it lacked the requisite small motor coordination, the years have passed, your adolescent has acquired a healthy respect for law and order, as well as the knowledge that, geographical distribution notwithstanding, Williams admits few freshmen from the juvenile house of detention. Your adolescent's solution, therefore, is to make its younger sibling run away from home, or at least beg to be sent to boarding school, preferably in Sri Lanka. To that end, your adolescent uses the methods of an est trainer, criticizing its younger sibling's taste, appearance, behavior, and eye color.

Not surprisingly, this creates difficulties for a parent. Every year when there is talk about who should receive the Nobel Peace Prize, thousands of mothers wonder why their names have not been mentioned—women who have laughed off shingles, Chapter Thirteen bankruptcy, and being in a plane that is about to ditch, women who wonder why Henry Kissinger made the front pages so often for the sort of shuttle diplomacy they practice every day.

Consider the mother who has invited her adolescent and its younger sibling to lunch at a restaurant. In many ways, this is relaxing for a mother. Focused as it is on its younger sibling, the adolescent momentarily is distracted from the main event. Thus, a parent actually may reach a table without having had it pointed out to her that (a) the table is not a good table, (b) she is speaking too loudly, or (c) she should have realized that when the adolescent said it wanted to go to lunch before, it didn't really mean it.

"Get your elbows off the table," hisses the adolescent to its sibling. Of course, this is precisely what Henry Kissinger was about to say, and theoretically he should be happy to have had his dirty work done for him. Unfortunately, Israel has delivered its criticism to little Egypt in a tone you might use at a car that has just made a right turn in front of you from the left lane.

"You always put your elbows on the table," continues Israel. "You have disgusting manners. It's mortifying to go anyplace with you."

"I do not," responds Egypt weakly. Suddenly it looks triumphant. "Anyway, at least I know enough to put my napkin on my lap."

"Gosh, you're right," says Israel, oozing contrition. Admission of error is Israel's secret weapon. It knows that Egypt has spent all week watching for a slip. It also knows that if it freely admits the gaffe, Egypt will have no place to go with it.

"What would you two like for lunch?" Henry Kissinger asks pleasantly, pointing out to Egypt that hamburgers are available and that the white rice is particularly tasty at this restaurant.

"What's the point of taking him to a restaurant when he can have hamburgers at home?" asks Israel, managing to get one off at Henry even as she gets another one off at Egypt.

"I just thought it would be pleasant to take both of you out for a nice lunch," says Henry. Diplomats like Henry Kissinger use words like "pleasant," "nice," and "fun" a great deal.

"Stop eating so much bread," says Israel to Egypt a bit later. "You won't be able to eat your hamburger."

In fact, Henry Kissinger was just about to tell Egypt the same thing. Seeing, however, that Egypt clearly is at least a squadron of fighter bombers behind, he leaps to Egypt's defense. "There's really no difference between bread and a hamburger roll," Henry points out.

"Egypt never finishes his food," Israel counters. "I hope you're not going to let him have dessert."

It happens that Henry Kissinger, who has had a weight problem all his life, is convinced that this is because his mother wouldn't let him have dessert until he finished all his meat. Henry Kissinger therefore has raised both Egypt and Israel so that they are permitted to have dessert even if they leave enough on their plate for Pakistan. For some reason, this has produced two paragons who never have had a weight problem, who frequently declare foods too rich, and whose idea of a good time is a chef's salad.[1]

Henry Kissinger unleashes his surefire ploy for bringing peace to the Middle East. "Of course Egypt may have dessert," he begins. "You two have such splendid nutritional habits only because I . . ." and continues on in the most boring way he knows how for at least two minutes, throwing in a lengthy reference to his own childhood.

"God," says Egypt.

"Oh, Henry," says Israel in disgust. Israel leans toward Egypt in comradely fashion. "There goes the United States again, talking about how much it's done for us."

Henry Kissinger knows that if there is anything guaranteed to unite two warring nations, it is a common enemy.

[1] Henry Kissinger always has regarded people who declare foods too rich with puzzled awe. In his entire life, Henry Kissinger never has encountered any food too rich.

Should This Material Be Protected by the First Amendment?

From: *Tiger Beat Star Super Special,* October/November, 1980

ERIK ESTRADA: HE'S FOOTLOOSE AND FANCY FREE—AGAIN!

Footloose is an adjective which means free to go where or do as one likes. These days, that's a perfect description of Erik!

ERIK's free again. Sadly, his marriage to Joyce Miller ended in divorce. Erik really wanted his marriage to work—he liked the idea of settling down with a wife and raising a family. Unfortunately, it just didn't happen that way.

That's in the past now. It's something Erik has to put behind him and go on. The fact is: Erik's a bachelor again! That means he can come and go as he pleases, and he doesn't have to consult with anyone before he makes a major decision. It also means Erik can date again!

If you're an Erik fan, even though you're sorry his marriage didn't work, you're probably pretty thrilled that he's free. Does that mean you have a chance with him again? Exactly!

* * *

You know in your heart it's bound to happen sooner or later—you want it too badly for it *not* to happen! And when that dream day finally dawns, are you going to be ready to meet your favorite star face to face? Well, TBSS wants to help make that day a day you'll remember forever—with a few hints on how to act when your impossible dream comes true at long last!

Star	*How to attract & catch him*
Michael Damian	Think young! Michael doesn't want to be old before his time, so don't be "too tired" to go out or think something is "too silly" to do. He loves shiny hair!
Ted Nugent	Be *very* unconventional but still feminine! *Don't* take drugs at all. Even in his wildest moments, don't be embarrassed or shy. Be outspoken!
Shawn Stevens	Be independent, but feminine. Be a good friend—kind, understanding and sincere. Love rollerskating.

* * *

Chris Atkins would always be ready to talk with you when you had a problem. He wouldn't want you to have to share it alone.

How to Discipline Your Adolescent Without Leaving Marks

Everybody knows that there are only two ways to get a small child to do something it doesn't want to do. These two methods are (1) bribes, and (2) threats.[1] The only people who appear not to know this are people who write books about how to raise children and who recommend, among other methods, reverse psychology. Reverse psychology is basically silly because it rests on a false premise. If your adolescent's room looks like the set of *Raise the Titanic*, that probably is not a reflection of its hostility toward you. By and large, your adolescent probably likes you and has a far more compelling rationale, e.g., choosing its clothes each morning from a pile on the floor provides it with more time to stare at the ceiling. Therefore, even assuming your child is not smart enough to see through a statement like "Oh, don't bother to clean up your room this week. I really don't care how it looks. In fact, it makes the rest of the house look neat by comparison"—which is to say, assuming your adolescent's IQ is below 85—reverse psychology will move your adolescent only to express pleasure at your finally having come around to seeing things its way.

Bribes and threats, on the other hand, continue to serve well during adolescence, although, as elsewhere, inflation has set in.

[1] Violence is merely a threat carried out.

Generally speaking, however, the promise of a car on its seventeenth birthday will propel almost any adolescent to clean up its room, and a great many will do their homework for a Betamax. Threats continue to be almost as effective, and while they occasionally cause some resentment, they do cost less than bribes. Threats must be considered, however. "I will kill you if you

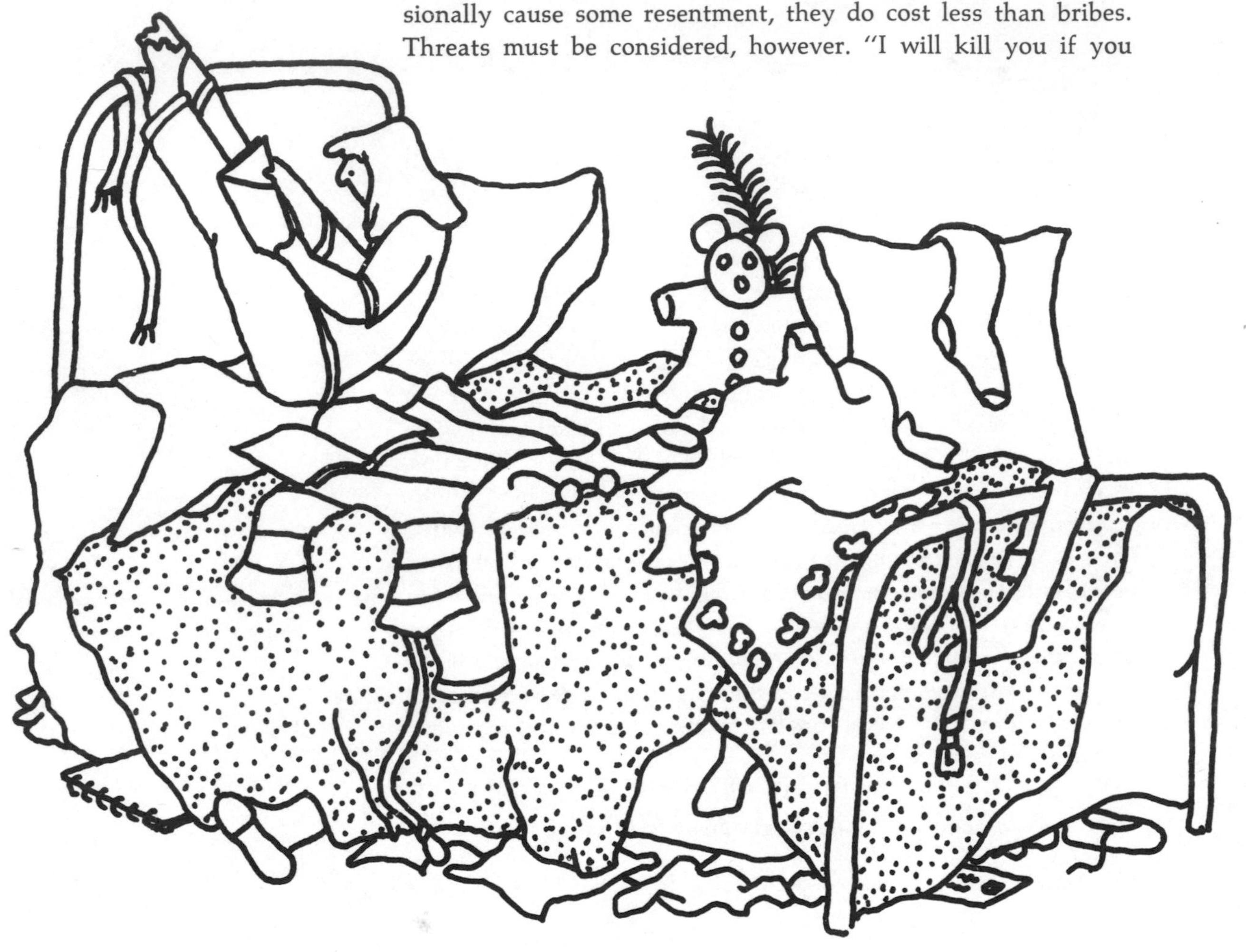

don't turn down that music" is not effective, since it lacks credibility. (Similarly, threats of bodily harm to someone who clearly can waste you.) Particularly difficult to deal with are adolescents whose *métier* is angst: "There's a probably really crummy party on Saturday but I don't want to hurt Jimmy's feelings so can I go?" In this instance, house arrest loses such force as a threat as to suggest the interesting question: Is it the adolescent who has in fact mastered reverse psychology?

Reason is a potent weapon but only if cleverly deployed. "If you don't clean up your room, you won't be able to find anything," says the unsophisticated parent, "and if you can't find anything, you won't be able to study efficiently." A vague and unsubstantiated argument never will shake your adolescent of its conviction that it is living in a fine residential hotel. If you cannot put Roy Cohn on retainer, remember that adolescents require proof—a report from the National Institutes of Health that heavy eye-makeup causes sudden unexplained weight gain, or a Gallup Poll showing that 90 per cent of those admitted to the College of Their Choice spent less than forty hours a week playing Dungeons and Dragons for two years prior to matriculation.

All things considered, reason probably is a better weapon than, say, threatening to run away from home, since it is unlikely your adolescent will lend you the plane fare. Strikes are apt to go unnoticed unless you have had the foresight to unplug the refrigerator. As for guilt, that is rather like the Atlas missile —effective but unpredictably messy.[2] "You know, when you were a baby you had diarrhea a lot" is hard not to say at times,

[2] One never knows whether the importunities to remember the starving children in India might not produce some years later a starving anorectic in Payne Whitney.

as is, "I divorced your father for that sort of thing." But best to leave guilt alone, since it is a weapon that carries with it the danger of falling into the wrong hands—i.e., your adolescent's. Adolescents, with their uncluttered little minds, are nonpareil at citing statistics on the effects on adolescents of processed baby foods, working mothers, being in a room with someone who smokes, and excessive television, which a parent who really cared would not have let it watch. "I didn't ask to be born in an era of rising unemployment, falling standard of living and the emergence of the United States as a second-rate power," your adolescent is likely to say to you.

In dealing with your adolescent, perhaps most important is that you learn to appreciate its sense of time and its less than optimistic view of foreign affairs. Thus, when you tell it to get a haircut and it answers with an enthusiastic "I will," and three weeks later you notice it having difficulty crossing streets because it cannot see through the hair covering its eyes, do not conclude that your adolescent is being mendacious. It is simply that time moves oddly for your adolescent—in the space of twenty-four hours it can have its life ruined forever by wearing the wrong belt and experience euphoria by receiving two invitations to go out on Saturday night. Three weeks can be the wink of an eye for your adolescent, who also believes, having been raised in parlous times, that at any moment the bomb may fall and wouldn't it be foolish to waste a trip to the barber?

Things to Think About While Waiting Up for Your Adolescent, Who Is Late

1. Is our society soft on crime?
2. Should the death penalty be reinstated for rapists, muggers, and people who exceed the speed limit by more than two miles an hour?
3. Has it ever conclusively been proven that marijuana smoking does not lead to heroin addiction?
4. Was Prohibition necessarily a bad thing?
5. Granted legalized abortion is a good thing, mightn't it be better if parental consent were required if the girl is younger than twenty-six?
6. Should the death penalty be reinstated for anyone who sells narcotics to those below the age of twenty-six?
7. Was the chastity belt necessarily a bad thing?
8. Should the driving age be raised to twenty-six?
9. If it weren't for affirmative action, would my child have an easier time getting admitted to the College of Its Choice?
10. Where are you, Barry Goldwater, now that we really need you?

Keep Out. No Trespassing. This Means You.

The CIA recently announced that it has been experiencing difficulty in recruiting. Many parents think this problem could be solved by broadening the search. "Loose lips sink ships" is the adolescent's motto. An adolescent on the subject of its right to privacy can wax more lyrical than a fund-raising letter from the ACLU.

This circumspectness regarding classified information extends, of course, to written communications as well. What your adolescent really wants for Christmas is its own security guard, or, failing that, a Mosler safe, the kind with the big round door they have inside banks. Your adolescent needs this sort of protection for its personal papers, e.g., old report cards, Playbills, dental check-up reminders. It has seen the same movies you have—movies in which wronged spouses steam open envelopes containing advertisements from record clubs.[1]

This passion for privacy stems in part from your adolescent's suspicion that becoming a person of mystery may revive occasionally flagging parental attention. Your adolescent has had it

[1] "What have you got in there?" asked one mother caught red-handed as she was innocently tidying the papers on her son's desk. "The plans for the atom bomb?" In fact, her son did have on his desk the plans for an atom bomb; he built a small one and was rewarded for his efforts with a scholarship to Princeton and a book contract.

with answering perfunctory questions about what it had for lunch while you read the evening paper and yawn. Intimations of a torrid seventh-grade liaison, the adolescent knows, will keep you awake at night thinking of nothing but itself.

Unfortunately for the CIA, adolescent discretion stops dead at the front door. Away from its immediate family, the typical adolescent makes the late Hubert Humphrey look like the late Calvin Coolidge. So burning is the adolescent's need to unburden itself to one of its own kind that it has developed a truly awesome instant-communications system. Example: One female adolescent whispered to her neighbor in the cafeteria line, "I'll kill you if you tell anybody, but I like Kenny." "I'll kill you if you tell . . ." is adolescent code for Broadcast Immediately, and when the adolescent reached her table, she was greeted with a bowl of green salad tossed over her head by Kenny's current girlfriend.

Keystone of the adolescent's communications system is the telephone. If an organization of adolescents were to award a medal for the greatest contribution to life as they know it, Alexander Graham Bell might not win (the inventor of the transistor certainly would give him a run for the money), but he would figure very strongly in the voting. Even the adolescent who is well versed in ancient history and who can conceive of life before electricity, automobiles, and decorator jeans really cannot believe that Julius Caesar did not receive his warning from the soothsayer via Dial-a-Horoscope.

Few adolescents have not at some point requested their own telephone. In part they do so to set a useful precedent for demanding a car of their own. In part they do so because they cannot be sure your phone is not tapped. In the main they do so because with a private telephone an adolescent need remove the

HOME
SECURITY
SYSTEMS

receiver from its ear only for mealtime, bedtime, and calls of nature, and, with an extra-long extension cord, not even then. If your adolescent has not agitated overmuch for its own private line, that probably is because it knows that in time you will feel the need for a telephone on which you yourself can make and receive calls and that you will run in a new private line of your own.

The telephone also serves as your adolescent's link to the main data bank, far more sophisticated than anything at the Department of the Census. By hooking into the data bank, your adolescent can inform you at any time of what Everybody Else is doing—buying forty-dollar sneakers, going to the skating party, having breast-augmentation surgery. Your adolescent also can inform itself of vital statistics—what color shoelaces are in fashion this week, what brand of breakfast cereal is being eaten only by creeps. If a fairy godmother were to offer to grant your adolescent one wish, the chances are that it would ask, "Please let me have no distinguishing marks or characteristics."[2]

[2] Some adolescents—fewer today than in the last decade or so—feel otherwise. They believe that to be similar in any way to any other adolescent or, indeed, to any other Earthling is a fate worse than having to listen to the Top Forty. This shall we say trying phenomenon is related to adolescent rebellion. Adolescents normally rebel by rejecting their parents' values and way of life—e.g., if you are a mogul, your adolescent will search for a career like that of Albert Schweitzer, only not that commercial. An interesting dilemma arises for some children of divorce, who are provided with no way to turn away from. Take Alison: Her mother, financial vice-president of a Fortune-500 company, yells, "Hit me again!" at the end of each eighty-hour week, and her father throws pots in New Mexico. You could gain forty-five pounds figuring what you're supposed to do to rebel. Probably Alison will become Elizabeth Holtzman.

Occasionally your curiosity will get the better of you and you will be tempted to snoop through your adolescent's mail, listen in on its phone calls, or purchase an electronic surveillance device. This is not only dishonorable but unnecessary. Stealthy younger siblings can be infected with a need to know as great as your own, and, more important, are hooked into the little brother–little sister network, where questions like "I'll tell you who my brother likes if you tell me who your sister likes" are SOP. You also might try telling your adolescent that you are writing a book on adolescents and that you need its help. Promise it a cut of the royalties if it gets you interviews with its friends. This has worked very nicely for me. Among other things, I found out who my son liked in the fifth grade.

As the years pass, your need to know will grow more intense. Does the fact that your adolescent asked you to buy Reddi Wip mean that it's hooked on nitrous oxide? Is your daughter being straight with you about toilet seats? Actually, there is no problem. As your mother often told you, you always can tell by looking in their eyes.

Like Story

Miles first glimpsed Priscilla in the seventh grade. "She's neat," he said to his best friend, John Alden, eyeing Priscilla's golden hair tucked under a Vegimals unicorn cap. "I think I'll ask her to the skating party next Saturday."

"You can't do that!" John said, horrified. John's older brother was an eighth-grader.

"I can't?" Miles asked, wounded. "Then how can I get to know her?"

"Leave it to me," answered John. Before his next class, he approached Priscilla's best friend, Hester, in the hall. "You know what I know? Miles likes Priscilla. Does she like him?" he asked after he had punched Hester on the arm. (In fact, John found Hester appealing, but he was not ready yet to declare his intentions.)

"Oh, yeah, sure, great," said Hester coolly, smoothing her baggy jeans.

"John said that Miles likes you," Hester reported excitedly to Priscilla after school that day on the phone.

"What should I do?" asked Priscilla, who had picked out Miles the moment they arrived in junior high as the boy she most wanted to listen to Pink Floyd with.

"Do nothing," Hester said, "but walk home from school with me tomorrow."

The next day, the two girls detoured on their way home from school so that they passed the field on which the seventh-grade boys practiced soccer. Priscilla caught sight of Miles. Miles caught sight of Priscilla. He kicked the ball away from John and brought it down the field, holding both hands behind his back and whistling "Eleanor Rigby." Priscilla looked away in disdain, her heart fluttering.

At school the next day, Miles walked over to Priscilla's locker and smashed her fingers in it. From then on everyone knew that Miles and Priscilla were an Item. For six months Priscilla and Miles did their math homework together on the telephone every night, and once Miles picked Priscilla up at her house when a group of their friends was going to a movie. ("Wasn't that a terrific movie?" Priscilla's mother, who already had seen it, asked her daughter. "I thought it was extremely well made," answered Priscilla.) This was noted in the annals of the seventh grade as a grand passion, and everyone was a little in awe.

In the ninth grade, Priscilla's mother asked Priscilla what ever happened to that nice Miles. "Gimme a break," said Priscilla disdainfully. "He's so immature. Can you imagine? He likes the BeeGees!"

"Fancy!" Priscilla's mother said. She wondered whether Priscilla might like to take dancing and piano lessons so that she could be a good dancer and play popular at parties. Priscilla's mother was a trifle concerned because Priscilla didn't date. She went to parties, it was true, and spent hours on the phone with her friends, making arrangements about when they would make plans for the weekend, but so far as boys went, Priscilla didn't seem to have a special fellow.

In fact, Priscilla had her hospital scrub-suit cap set on Danny, John's older brother in the tenth grade, even though Hester said Danny kissed wet. Priscilla wasn't quite sure how to get Danny

interested. She wasn't in any of his classes, so she couldn't pass him notes that said, "Hi! How are you? 'Bye!" She couldn't call him up to ask about homework assignments. Priscilla considered becoming manager of the basketball team, but then she decided the school paper was less likely to ruin her fingernails. She put on her "Pardon me, but you've obviously mistaken me for someone who gives a damn" T-shirt to get things off on the right foot.

Priscilla and Danny discovered they liked all the same things. Their favorite authors were J. R. R. Tolkien and Stephen King, their favorite music was New Wave, their favorite movie scene the open-heart surgery scene in *All That Jazz,* their favorite sneakers Adidas. Priscilla and Danny often could be seen strolling together, their earphones connected to Danny's Sony Walkman, pressing the Hot Line button that connected them to each other. "Plastic, commercial, and bland," Priscilla would say. "Essentially dumb," Danny would echo.

Often Danny visited Priscilla at her house, where Priscilla's mother heard them whispering softly about lithium batteries and cross-over distortion as they fitted a new diamond needle to Priscilla's stylus, which Priscilla's mother never, never, never touched. Other than that, Priscilla's mother noticed, they didn't seem to talk very much.

Finally, Priscilla's mother asked Priscilla why Danny never escorted her to a party. Patiently, Priscilla explained that a boy did not escort a girl to a party; he just spent his time with her when they were there, and when everybody went to a concert or to *The Rocky Horror Show* he sat next to her.

"I don't get it," Priscilla's mother said. "What do you call what you and Danny are doing?"

"It's called Going Out," Priscilla answered gently.

"But you don't go anywhere unless you're with twelve other people," Priscilla's mother said.

"That's okay," Priscilla responded. "I'm going out with Danny so I can't go out with anyone else."

"There are advantages to playing the field, you know," Priscilla's mother said.

Priscilla looked horrified. "What kind of a girl do you think I am?" she asked.

In tenth grade, Priscilla felt secure enough with Danny to call him on the telephone and to stop saying, "How fascinating!"

when he took her to a basketball game. But Priscilla's mother began to worry. Priscilla was losing weight. (Priscilla and her friends had discovered that they could induce vomiting by chewing up old Farrah Fawcett-Majors posters and swallowing them.)

"What happened to that nice Danny?" Priscilla's mother asked her one night. Priscilla burst into tears.

"He's a fascist," she said. "Last month he wore a T-shirt that said 'Nuke the Whales,' and last week he wore one that said 'I have no opinion about nuclear energy.' And yesterday he wore a T-shirt that said absolutely nothing at all, which means he's not even talking to me."

"I don't understand," Priscilla's mother said.

"He told me I had no appreciation of literature because I didn't like the scene in *The World According to Garp* where she cuts out his liver and throws it fifty yards away," Priscilla sobbed. "And when I told him I didn't like Aerosmith because their lyrics are so disgustingly sexist he said he thought we ought to start seeing other people." Danny, Priscilla reported, had given her back her Christmas present, a key chain made from brick salvaged from the childhood home of Janis Joplin.

Perhaps if Priscilla were more vivacious, her mother thought. In her own day she had been adept at saying smart, funny things to boys to get their attention and then giggling so they wouldn't think she was smart. But Priscilla's generation seemed to have decided that expressing enthusiasm of any sort caused premature wrinkling. It took Priscilla's mother several months to get over her daughter's romance.

Your Adolescent's First Affair: A Sample Menu

Three things in life are certain: death, taxes, and that one day early in its adolescence your adolescent will want to throw a party. In fact, the certainty of the first two is open to debate: the science of cryogenics is developing rapidly, as is the art of finding in the Internal Revenue Code what some call loopholes and others call triumphant archways. Nothing, however, is in the offing that will prevent the third.

Prepare for the event and for learning your part in it (provider-pariah) by scouting a party at another adolescent's home. The easiest way to do that is to arrange to fetch your own adolescent. (You need not arrive early; whenever you arrive will be early.) Notice on entering that although the music is being played at a volume favored by Savak for getting subversives to confess, the screaming can be heard clearly above the music, and the giggling can be heard clearly above the screaming. Now find the host parent and ask him or her how many adolescents are in there.[1] Provided the parent has not yet been reduced to a state of babbling incoherence, you will get an answer; the number quoted will be approximately one third of your estimate.

[1] Even in the most nuclear of families more than one parent rarely will be in attendance. The other has promised to transfer all the AT&T into joint names or to change the cat's litter box for the next twenty years in order to be excused.

You may have difficulty locating the parent; try looking in a closet. One picking-up mother was ushered quickly into a bedroom to meet her opposite number, a wild-eyed woman with trembling hands. Probably an alcoholic, thought the visitor, who had not yet chaperoned a party herself. "I'd offer you a cup of coffee," quavered the resident mother, "but I'm not allowed to go through to the kitchen again for another twenty minutes." "Oh," said the guest's mother, edging toward the door, "that's perfectly all right."[2]

Adolescent parties are of several varieties, but central to all of them is food. Figure on one quart of ice cream (sprinkles are crucial), one quart of milk, and one one-liter bottle of Coke per guest.[3] Also, one pound per guest of any mixture of the following:

Mint Milanos
Weight Watchers Apple Treats
M&M's
Chocolate-chip cookies
Strawberry Pop-Tarts
Reese's Peanut Butter Cups
Nutter Butter Cookies
Potato chips, popcorn, pretzels
Doritos, Tostitos, Fritos

Also essential is the proper setting. Your adolescent will expect you to have the house appropriately neat and clean, which is to say adequate for inspection by an adoption agency. Repainting

[2] Explained the visitor's son to her later: "I wanted you to see what it was like when you took me to visit one of your friends who had a kid and you told us to go play."

[3] Or one one-liter bottle of Pepsi, depending on whether you prefer to overhear the guests cackling, "No Cuk, Pepsi" or "No Pepsi, Cuk."

and reupholstering probably are in order. Now is the time to buy that wall-to-wall carpeting you were thinking about or, better, to move.

In return for promising to let your adolescent choose what you will wear, it may agree to tell you what kind of party it plans to

have and how many guests it expects. Don't forget to double that figure.[4] Probably the party will be one of the following:

The Dinner Party

Pizza is *de rigueur.* Your adolescent will supply you with the name of the right pizza caterer. As the wrong omelet man once ruined a party for your best adult friend, so the wrong pizza parlor will spell social disaster for your thirteen-year-old. Discourage the dinner party if you can, since integral to it is the food fight, which generally begins when someone does something disgusting—e.g., inserting a small piece of everything edible (see list above) into a soda can. Another person does the same, then another. Soon afterward somebody spills, then somebody else spills, and about that time somebody else discovers that a fork makes a terrific slingshot. And there you are—or will be the next morning—preparing to reupholster again.

The Necking Party

By this is not meant the sort of party that takes place when there is no parent about, which is not exactly a necking party. The true adolescent necking party is not common, but it begins when one of the sweeter guests says, "Hey, I'll bet your parents would like it if we played Spin the Bottle. My mother got all misty-eyed when we did that at my party." When the parent, recognizing the unmistakable nervous giggles of her youth, emerges from her closet, the adolescents stop the game with relief.

[4] This information also will come in handy when you're fielding inquiries from parents of invited guests. Have available as well your D&B rating, the year in which your ancestors emigrated to this country, and a plausible explanation for your membership during college in any organization to the left of the Young Republicans.

The Silent Party

The action here revolves around an electronic game that has been hooked up to your television set in such a way that you will never be able to get Channel 7 again. If you leave your closet to observe this pastime, you will find alive in the room only little white dots on the screen and thumbs.

The Party

Except for the noise and confusion more closely associated with children's birthday parties or the Tokyo subway, the basic adolescent party seems at first very much like an adult party—people dance, people talk, people eat. The major difference is that adolescent guests have no compunctions about announcing that they are bored or about telling the host or hostess that he or she should figure out something else for them to do. The problem is that no group of more than three adolescents wants to do the same thing at the same time. They cannot split up into, say, one group for charades and another for dancing, however, because the host or hostess feels that if it were a good party, everybody would be having fun doing the same thing at the same time. It is this that often makes the atmosphere of an adolescent party resemble that of a Marine boot camp.[5]

Your role in all this is simple: to refill the potato-chip bowls and, if necessary, to empty the punch bowl, with the unobtrusiveness of a butler at an English country-house weekend. Under no circumstances say, "Why don't you . . . ?" As you cower in your closet, derive some comfort from the knowledge that no

[5] It is also this that makes adolescents better chaperones than their parents. It is the adolescent who notices first and brings back into the fold six guests who suddenly have conceived a desire for fresh air on a night when there is a hailstorm or who are unusually willing to carry garbage out to the incinerator.

matter how many of its friends tell your adolescent its party was the social event of the decade, it will be so convinced the party was a disaster because of the way you came in with the Tostitos that it will not schedule another party until next year. As for the year after that, the Party will have gone the way of the Lootbag, and you will lie awake waiting for your adolescent to return home from Getting Together.

Clear Days on the Psychiatric Scene

From *Normal Adolescence,* formulated by the committee on adolescence of the Group for the Advancement of Psychiatry.[1]

> "Boys defend against [castration anxiety] in various ways. For example, some boys become fearful of any kind of body injury and behave passively, avoiding physical activity and roughhouse games; others unconsciously deny their fears and plunge headlong into activities which tend to be daring or risky. . . ."

1 "In this chapter, the discussion will be focused on the dynamics of the internal psychological (intrapsychic) functioning of the adolescent and his closer relationships with people (object relationships)."

Deciphering the Dress Code

You might think from what you read in the papers, not to mention in the Constitution, that the United States is a democracy. If you think that, that is because you have not spent much time with your adolescent and its peers. Class distinctions among adolescents make the British aristocracy look like Plato's Retreat. Probably the closest analogy is to the India of a century ago.

The primary manifestation of the adolescent caste system is the adolescent dress code. Until the late 1960s, many schools, both public and private, had dress codes.[1] During the late great unpleasantness, dress codes were jettisoned along with other anachronisms, e.g., learning to read, grades below C. Always ready to step in and fill a vacuum, however, the adolescents themselves proceeded to devise a dress code of far greater rigidity and with far more severe penalties for deviation. (What is being sent home from school to get your hair cut compared with knowing that until you figure out what is wrong with your socks, no one will eat lunch with you?)

The primary purpose of the dress code is to make it unnecessary for the already overburdened adolescent to waste time figuring out who is worth knowing. It is rather as if you were pro-

[1] At one private school in New York, where a boy attending classes in a tie and jacket nowadays is treated gingerly by his peers because it is assumed he is on his way to or from a funeral, there once was a lady whose primary function was to check students' hands for dirty fingernails.

vided in advance with the curriculum vitae of every guest at a large cocktail party. The following list will be useful for you if you must outfit an adolescent recently arrived from six years in the bush.

The Preppie

Preppies are easy to identify. You definitely own one if your old Brooks Brothers crew-necks keep disappearing.[2] Girl preppies look pretty much the way their mothers looked if their mothers went to Vassar and were friendly with girls named Mopsy, Muffie, Buffy, Betsy, and Bitsy. (So perfectly retrograde is the fashion analogy, in fact, that if you never have stopped dressing that way, you now can save money by shopping in your local Junior department.) Girl preppies buy less by label than by location. "I picked this up in the country" is how the preppie answers an inquiry about her wardrobe, the country being a place like Southampton or Nantucket. A preppie's hair is ideally dark blond and is never set; it is washed daily, preferably at 6:00 A.M. so that it will dry before school without having to be slept on.

Boy preppies look much the way their fathers did if they dated girls in college named Mopsy et cetera. The boy preppie wears La Coste shirts (except they are now called Izods) or button-downs (except they are now called Oxfords), chinos or jeans, and letter sweaters. White bucks and Madras jackets are on the horizon, as also may be the Young Americans for Freedom.

The Jap

Originally the acronym for Jewish American Princess, the ap-

[2] To be a second-generation preppie accords high status. "This is my mother's circle pin, she wore it at Smith," is a very good thing to be able to say.

pellation now admits everyone regardless of race, creed, or color. In training via Fiorucci for Vuitton and Gucci, the jap is the person for whom designer jeans were invented. (Laminated onto her body is the fit she is after.) The jap, who for her graduation from high school wants a Tank Watch, has both bone and white sandals and is tan all year round. She buys outfits rather than clothes, and the nice thing about her is that if you see her lying for hours on her bed staring up at the ceiling, you can be fairly sure she is not thinking about suicide but rather about accessoriz-

ing or about transitional cottons. Those japs who want to associate with preppies or normals (see below) try to explain their predilection ("Levi's just don't fit me"), but most feel people should take them as they are: with their gold jewelry, their relatively restrained eye-makeup (a touch of mascara, liner, and powder-blue shadow), and their blusher, which they apply with a trowel.

Boy japs look very much like preppies except that (a) their clothes are inappropriately pressed; (b) their blazers have the wrong linings; (c) they have not mastered the art of tying a crew-neck sweater around the neck, often dropping it, in case you always wondered how they get lost.

The Punk

Because punks of both sexes dress like their favorite performer, the precise formulation is difficult to describe, as is any given punk's gender. Generally, however, punks favor black shirts and avoid any article of clothing that might be worn by a preppie or a jap, unless they can put their individual stamp on the outfit—e.g., a down jacket worn with bare feet, an alligator shirt worn with bondage pants, a girls'-school uniform worn with combat boots. The punk sees its hair as an outlet for expressing its personality, coloring it to match its clothes or enlivening it with a stripe or two. Makeup runs to sequins and sparkles, and if we truly are returning to the fifties, by the time you read this, female punks will be wearing fishnet stockings and antique lace shirts.

The Parkie

The parkie hangs out in parks and wears torn jeans and Army jackets and throws a Frisbee. It is the combination of Army jacket and Frisbee-throwing that is key, since otherwise parkies might be confused with punks. Both parkies and punks often are confused. Those who are into downward mobility often carry large boxes for the soon-to-be-hearing-impaired.[3]

The Normal

The normal appears to think less than the other types about clothes; in fact, as the true nonconformist of its generation, it spends vast amounts of energy and time trying to "look good" without falling into any category. This is very hard. A female normal, for example, eschewing blusher because that is jap, will stand on her head and hang upside down to get color into her cheeks. So unremarkable is the normal's appearance that it runs the danger of being confused with the schlepp (or nerd, see below). The differences are in the normal's clothes (they fit) and in the normal's choice of sneakers. Like all adolescents except schlepps, the normal recognizes the importance of sneakers in forging one's sense of self. After all, it wears sneakers 100 per cent of the time except when it goes to the opera. Therefore, the adolescent has developed the ability to discriminate among a hundred pairs of sneakers displayed on a wall. "I like those," it will say, pointing to one pair. "Those are disgusting," it will say, pointing to another pair that to the adult appears identical.[4] Also worn extensively by the normal, as well as by other types of adolescent, is the imprinted T-shirt. A reason for the drop in

[3] If someday your life depends (and it may) on telling the difference between a parkie and a punk, the former favor the Grateful Dead, the latter the Sex Pistols.

[4] Usually what it likes is that Rolls Royce of sneakers, Adidas. One adolescent girl, accosted by a large adolescent boy who demanded her money, said, "What do you need my money for? You've got a down jacket and Adidas," and walked on unscathed.

SAT verbal scores over the past two decades may be that adolescents now communicate primarily via T-shirts.[5]

The Schlepp (var. Nerd)

Schlepps, generally either extremely brilliant or incredibly stupid, are the adolescent underclass; nobody wants to be with them because it might rub off. The abrupt changes in adolescent fashion may in fact be caused when an acutely sensitive jap notices that a schlepp has just bought a pair of baggy jeans, which means that baggy jeans suddenly are Out.

At the bottom of the underclass are schlepps who do nothing but study and who are called grinds (a remarkably durable word, no?). No matter what your type of adolescent, it considers being known as a grind worse than having its parents show its nude baby pictures to a date. Reputations can be made or broken on the basis of how many books an adolescent is seen carrying home from school.

Despite the caste system, most adolescents are democratic enough to mix occasionally at large school functions with those who are not Their Kind, and even to discuss homework assignments. Parties, of course, remain segregated, and no adolescent would consider Going Out with somebody not of its caste. Therein lies anarchy, confusion, and the necessity for getting to know what another person really is like.

[5] E.g., "I don't know. I don't care. And it doesn't make any difference"; "It's not that you and I are so clever, but that others are such fools"; "SO?"; "Ignore alien orders"; "I know you think you understood what I said, but what you heard was not what I meant."

Your Questions about Adolescence Answered

Q. I am worried that my adolescent may be schizophrenic. I have been receiving disturbing reports from those who have entertained him for a weekend. Typical is: "Jonathan was wonderful, what a charming fellow, such an outgoing personality, he just kept us laughing all through dinner, that wonderful cheese soufflé he whipped up, and I can't tell you what I'd give to see our Malcolm with manners like that." The last time Jonathan uttered more than a grunt in my presence was six months ago when I dusted his turntable, and I have to hold him at knife point to get him to write a thank-you note. I have checked and he is the only Jonathan who visited that weekend.

A. Relax. Remember the baby-sitter who told you when you got home how nicely your children played together and how they helped her with the dishes at a time when even if you could have got them to help you with the dishes, you wouldn't have, because you would have worried too much that one child would break a glass on the counter and use the shards to permanently disfigure the other? Your adolescent is not schizophrenic. It is just that its sense of what it can get away with where has reached a level unequaled by most Presidents of the United States.

Q. I myself do not have an adolescent, but some of my best friends do. What should I talk to an adolescent about? And how can I learn to speak Adolescent?

A. Music is always a good topic, as is sound equipment. "What do you think of the new STA 7M full-featured receiver rated at 10 watts per channel, minimum RMS into 4 ohms from 20–20,000 Hz, with no more than 1 per cent total distortion?" will get you an adolescent's attention, although its parents may not invite you back. If you want to conduct a more extensive dialogue, try current events: "What do you think about Stevie Nicks leaving Fleetwood Mac?" although here you run the risk that this particular adolescent may feel that Teenage Jesus and the Jerks is the only group worth listening to. It may be safer, therefore, to study beforehand that favorite adolescent news weekly, the *National Enquirer.* "What do you think about that priest's body that was perfectly preserved after ninety-three years in an open tomb?" is the sort of thing that makes a good opener.

As for speaking Adolescent, it's easy if you're willing to spend the time—about the same as taking an advanced degree in thermodynamics. An inattentive adolescent, however, can be made to think you have a so-to-speak nodding acquaintance with the language if you will follow a few simple rules: (1) Never speak in complete sentences; (2) Never speak more than six words without inserting a "y'know" or a "like"; (3) Substitute the word "goes" for the word "says" whenever possible, as in "So I go, 'You can't do that, y'know, to me.' And he goes, 'Like what do you mean, girl?' "

Interestingly enough, not all adolescents speak Adolescent. A substantial minority speak English and are willing to suffer the taunts of their peers, who complain that they are "glib." A small group of adolescents speaks Haut Adolescent and thinks William Safire is a disgrace to the language. Speakers of this dialect often are found in the company of younger siblings, whose split infinitives they pounce upon with haut satisfaction. Parents also are treated to the purism of such adolescents, who seem to live for the misplaced parental modifier. Conversations like this one, which occurred outside a front door, are symptomatic:

Sibling: Does everyone have their key?
Adolescent: Does everyone have *his* key, Stupid.
Mother: Does everyone have his or her key, actually.
Adolescent: His or her is acceptable nowadays in writing but not in idiomatic speech.
Sibling: Mommy, do you have your key? Billy, do you have your key?

Q. My adolescent is only twelve years old but says it is too old for a baby-sitter. I am nervous and want to continue to have baby-sitters. What should I do?

A. Be honest with your adolescent about your fears. Tell it how you are afraid that there might be an emergency and it might get injured, or that someone might break in, or that there will be a newspaper story about you with a headline that reads: "Child Killed in Apartment House Fire. Left Alone by Bad Mommy."

Q. Is there such a thing as adolescent angst?

A. It is difficult to know whether adolescent angst is real or whether it should be filed with the myth that men are not fit to hold public office because of their raging hormonal cycles. That is because it is difficult ever to know how your adolescent feels.

Unless it received a psychoanalyst as a gift last Christmas, your adolescent is hampered in its ability to describe its emotional state. The primary cause, a deficient vocabulary, will be remedied when your adolescent enters college and returns home on Thanksgiving convinced it has every neurosis in its psychology text. Until that time, however, your adolescent probably will admit to only two emotional states. These are (1) bored and (2) okay. That does not mean that your adolescent is never happy. It is just that your adolescent knows it is bad public relations ever to permit you to see it happy. It wants to keep you on your toes.

Q. My adolescent spends most of its time at a friend's house. I have checked and the friend's mother usually serves tuna-noodle casserole for dinner, the same as I do. Also, she does not have braided and feathered hair or wear a hospital scrub suit. Why is she popular and I'm not?

A. You can become popular with your adolescent's friends by stocking a complete selection of Nabisco cookies and by lending them your American Express card. But none of this will make you a popular Mommy to your own adolescent because you are its Mommy, so try adopting one of its friends whom you like or telling your own adolescent it is adopted.

Q. Lately I have noticed that my adolescent stares at the ceiling for hours on end. Is this anything to be concerned about, and do you have any idea what it is thinking about?

A. Staring at a ceiling is completely normal adolescent behavior and cause for concern only when you no longer can clean around it. Every adolescent thinks about different things while it is staring at the ceiling, although many of them think about whether there is a God and about the metaphysical bases for acne. Parents of adolescents also think about God. I, for instance, have decided that every year God chooses fifty Nielsen families to test and that this year I am one.

Fun With Your New Symptom

No adolescent likes to be felled by a loathsome disease, or even by a relatively attractive one, but assuming the illness is benign—e.g., the mass-absence virus teachers slip into the cafeteria food early in February—your adolescent is willing to make the best of it. Your adolescent realizes there are worse things in life (Chemistry tests spring to mind) than spending a few days catching up with Laura and Leslie on *General Hospital*, not to mention being waited on by its mother hand and foot. True, it is difficult to get your mother to serve you an appetizing luncheon of Mint Milanos and strawberry Pop-Tarts, but the resourceful adolescent knows that if it complains about feeling nauseated, it can get a Coke, and that if it wants ice cream, all it has to do is to mention incessantly its sore throat.[1]

A proper diet, of course, is only the beginning of getting everything the adolescent wants, although the service never equals what it got with its childhood diseases, when the TV set was wheeled to its bedside, when whole toy stores were deposited on

[1] Assume a mother not employed outside the home, as in the story of the missionary and the economist who were thrown into a pit filled with alligators. "What will we do?" screamed the missionary. "No problem," answered the economist calmly. "Assume a ladder." Note that I avoid the locution "non-working mother." That is because the hardest job I ever held was exclusive mothering. The phrase "non-working mother" is a contradiction in terms; the phrase "working mother" is redundant.

its sickbed, when Mommy read *The Little Engine That Could* six times in a row. The major benefit of an illness during adolescence is that it functions as calling in sick does for an adult—no school, no homework, no taking out the garbage. Small wonder that convalescence often is protracted.

For some adolescents, it is this appreciation of the benefits of delicate health that underlies their hypochondria. The only other group that monitors its health with such attention is patients in intensive-care units.[2] Other adolescents' hypochondria stems from a belief in divine retribution that might have struck Cotton Mather as excessive. Despite the fact that every book, pamphlet, and seventh-grade health teacher has reassured them that everything up to and including having a meaningful relationship with a chicken is normal and nothing is left that causes hair to grow on the palms of the hands, many adolescents persist in believing that, say, having missed one food today from the four basic food groups probably is fatal and they will die and go to Hell.

Still other adolescents enjoy hypochondria but cultivate stoicism. "I keep having this funny thing in my throat where I can't breathe," says the adolescent. "Really?" asks the alarmed parent. "How long have you had it?" "About a year," says the adolescent, who did not bother to mention the symptom at last week's annual check-up because it didn't seem important at the time. This somewhat cavalier attitude causes many parents to be less than sympathetic. "Oh," they say, "probably just your old brain tumor kicking up again. Can I have your coin collection?" Although tempting, making light of your adolescent's symptoms is not recommended; it may result in a call from the high-school

[2] The only other being that receives the scrutiny your adolescent focuses on its own body is Best in Breed at the Westminster Kennel Club Show.

nurse saying that, despite everything Robert has told her about your attitude toward his health, she feels you really ought to be informed that he just broke his collarbone.

If they do not impress parents, the adolescent's illnesses and injuries are at least useful among its peer group. They can engender envy—"Oh, you lucky!" its fellows say as they gather around the person who has managed to miss two pop quizzes. Illnesses can confer an air of mystery—being the first to contract this season's flu confers high status on an adolescent, as does any condition its colleagues cannot pronounce or spell—and of romance. Nobody reads *The Magic Mountain* any longer, but the allure of rare diseases endures. Ski injuries and anything at all acquired outside the continental United States probably are the best, since they permit even the most modest adolescent to keep its status vacation in the minds of its peers for weeks or months.

The true diseases of adolescence, however, are The Pimple, The Shortness, and The Fatness. "Well," sighed one five-foot-four-inch fourteen-year-old boy who had grown only three inches in the past year, "I guess I'll just have to resign myself to being short, where do we keep the rat poison?" Pointing out to it that its parents' average height was five-eleven and that both had been dwarfs until their sixteenth year had of course no effect. Adolescents know they will never Outgrow It. How can you trust a person who tells you you can lose weight by cutting down on starches? The adolescent knows that its only hope is to find a miracle cure, which is why companies that manufacture nostrums for The Pimple are immune to market fluctuations. "Where do you think we should go this summer?" asked one mother, in a last-ditch effort to distract her daughter, who had just canceled all social engagements for a month because of the appearance of a delicate pinkish spot on her chin. "How about Lourdes?" suggested the adolescent.

Beating the (School) System

"Why am I still here?" your adolescent wonders. It can read the sports pages, use a pocket calculator, order in a French restaurant. It has received sex education in the sixth, seventh, and ninth grades (the eighth presumably was left open for independent study). Why, then, does your adolescent return to school every fall instead of joining Hare Krishna or the Century Association? Not only because it has decided that, outside of *General Hospital*, daytime TV doesn't really hold up. Primarily because its friends are there, and because it has by now discovered the satisfactions of beating the system.[1]

[1] It is possible that you will get an adolescent who has not yet mastered beating the system, quite the contrary, and this may worry you. It should not. The primary purpose of post-grade-school education is to prevent able-bodied workers from flooding the economy. A certain amount of intellectual exercise is provided to the brain by one or two subjects, notably mathematics. Otherwise, for the most part, students are kept busy memorizing material that will seep out of their heads as soon as they have blackened in the last circle with their number-two pencil. ("I don't see how this is going to help my daughter find a husband," I have been tempted to say more than once to her teachers.) The same analytic faculties are brought into play by the adolescent who owns two thousand records and can discern the differences among the Grateful Dead, the Talking Heads, and the Dead Boys or comprehend the meaning of the lyrics of "My Clone Sleeps Alone." The only problem is that certain colleges have not yet discovered this equation and insist on silly things like good grades and the ability to not nod off during admissions interviews. But, as

Consider an average day for an average adolescent sociopath whom we shall call Kimberly. Having brought her brain up to optimum cruising speed by successfully outwitting her mother's attempts to make her eat breakfast, Kimberly arrives at school ten or twenty minutes early. The time before classes begin Kimberly spends walking around talking to her friends (not unlike a cocktail party), or sprawled on the floor talking to her friends (not unlike a loft party), or making dates for lunch in the cafeteria (not unlike a dinner party). In fact, Kimberly has decided, school is rather like a social club with a few catches.

The major catch, of course, is the teaching staff. Having studied teachers for most of her life, Kimberly has decided they can be divided loosely into two types: Plumbers and Others. Most of Kimberly's teachers have been plumbers, people Kimberly sincerely believes would have made excellent plumbers or rock stars or nuclear physicists, but who never should have become teachers. Miss Baldwin, who teaches English and is a typical plumber, generally arrives about fifteen minutes late and spends ten more trying to unlock her desk before she begins the class with a story about her poodle. Fortunately, Miss Baldwin places

---

they say, there is a college for every student, perhaps Bowling Green University in Kentucky, the only institution of higher learning in the country with a Popular Culture Department. Reports *Rolling Stone:* "'A McDonald's golden arch can be as representative to me of the Garden of Eden as the frontier to a historian,' declares Ray B. Browne, founder of the Popular Culture Association and chairman of the department. In Introduction to Popular Culture, Browne and his students pore over torchy novels, perform in-class soap operas and take an occasional field trip. 'We watch people coming into a fast-food place,' says Browne, 'and observe the rituals they go through. Then we question them: "Were you aware you were doing this?" And they say, "I don't know, I was just coming in to get a hamburger."'"

so high a value on good conversation, she appears not to mind that her lecture is viewed by her students as static. Kimberly uses the time to catch up with those friends she missed before class, to look at a boy across the room until he looks at her and then to look quickly away from him and into her compact mirror, and to ponder whether she should choose politics or journalism as her major in extracurricular activities. Kimberly has analyzed in the school's computer the dossier of every student from her school who was admitted to the College of Her Choice during the last five years. The best bets seem to be high SATs, presidency of the student council, and a family that practices Zoroastrianism.

In Mr. Davis's Biology class Kimberly queries a neighbor about whether she should run for class president, whether a light turnout would help her, and what planks to put into her platform for the jocks. Mr. Davis, also a plumber, announces a test for Friday; Kimberly sighs. Mr. Davis gives very hard tests.[2] The students, however, have given up on Mr. Davis, and Kimberly continues her conversation. When she hears through the din an unfamiliar word, she asks her neighbor, "That's in the book, isn't it?"

It is much the same in Mrs. Cole's French class, which Kimberly decides to use as a study hall, since Study Hall is reserved for a quick trip to Burger King.[3] Why did Mrs. Cole become a

[2] Mr. Davis is the sort who gives optional homework assignments for the "more motivated" students. "I am not motivated," Kimberly answered her father when he asked why she didn't do those questions. "I am just smart."

[3] Except on Wednesdays when Study Hall turns into Health, the perennial euphemism for sex education. Since there is little more to impart to the children about sex (*ménage à trois* and necrophilia being about the only two variations that have not been thoroughly described), this year the unit is on alcohol, which has, of course, been

French teacher? Kimberly muses. She never has even visited France, probably because, with her accent, she is afraid people will laugh and point at her.

At least Kimberly has no trouble deciding what her History teacher should have been. Mrs. Peyser should have been Abbie Hoffman. Mrs. Peyser's view of History has been influenced strongly by the civil rights movement of the sixties, the Vietnam protest movement of the seventies, and the women's liberation, gay liberation, anti-nuclear, Save the Whales, and Impeach Justice Rehnquist movements along the way. Kimberly has learned that if she answers every essay question on Mrs. Peyser's History tests as though she just has been hit over the head by a policeman, she will do okay.

The only Other that Kimberly has this year is Mr. Meisel. There is nothing extraordinary about Mr. Meisel or about Intermediate Algebra, except that Mr. Meisel comes in, does his job, and leaves. When Mr. Meisel was studying to be a teacher, Kimberly has decided, somebody gave him a step-by-step manual on teaching, a good one, and he has followed it ever since. No variations, no surprises. If there is one thing Kimberly hates, it is surprises. For Kimberly has discovered that once having figured a teacher out, she can give that teacher what he or she wants and that teacher will give Kimberly what she wants—a grade that will make up for her lack of Zoroastrianism without causing her to work so hard that schoolwork interferes with her life. Once Kimberly asked her parents, who have given up eating so that they can afford to send Kimberly to a good private school

---

covered twice before. "But what have they got left to *teach* you?" cries Kimberly's mother. "I don't know," says Kimberly. "Maybe how to make a Harvey Wallbanger."

where for a mere five thousand dollars a year their daughter can receive the same education they got for free twenty-five years ago, a question:

"If they tell you in nursery school that you have to work hard so that you'll do well in kindergarten, and if they tell you in kindergarten that you have to work hard so you'll do well in elementary school, and if they tell you in elementary school that you have to work hard so you'll do well in high school, and if they tell you in high school that you have to work hard so you'll get into a good college, and assuming that they tell you in college that you have to work hard so you'll get into a good graduate school, what do they tell you in graduate school that you have to work hard for?"

"To get a good job so that you can make enough money to send your children to a good nursery school," Kimberly's parents answered.

Aid for the Busy Parent

Being the parent of an adolescent is a full-time job. But sometimes you need a rest. Wouldn't you know that just when you need a rest most, your adolescent decides it needs you? Here are eighteen surefire sentences guaranteed to get your adolescent to go back to watching *Love Boat* and to leave you alone.

1. Time heals all wounds.
2. You'll outgrow it.
3. You'll get over it.
4. It's your glands.
5. It's just a phase you're going through.
6. Someday you'll be happy you have a little sister. She'll have lots of nice friends you can date.
7. Someday you'll be happy you have a big brother. He'll have lots of nice friends you can date.
8. When I was your age I had an allowance of [insert any number], and all my friends envied me.
9. When I was your age [insert any phrase].
10. Your thighs are perfect.
11. I can't see anything wrong with your face.
12. Don't be ridiculous; nobody will notice.
13. It's your inner beauty that really counts; someday you'll meet a boy/girl who sees that and is worthy of you.

14. Smile and the world smiles with you.
15. I think it's time we had a discussion about [insert any subject].
16. Stand up straight.
17. These are the happiest years of your life.
18. Give me a hug.

The Total Adolescent

Many feminist mothers worry about how to raise their daughters. They assume that they should not raise their daughters as their mothers raised them. I myself am not at all sure what my own mother raised me to be, and because she long since has gone to that great bridge game in the sky, I probably never will know.

I do know that I never was taught how to cook, clean, or iron. Neither was I told there was no need to know such things because of my destiny as an otolaryngologist or a prima ballerina. Not that my mother was idle. She taught me how to arrange flowers, where to place the fish fork, the difference between real and fake engraving, and never to wear white after Labor Day. Now that I think of it, I probably was raised to be a rich man's plaything—about the only thing, as fate would have it, that I have not become.

I was pondering all this one day in, where else, Bloomingdale's, where I had taken my daughter to shop for school clothes. Also shopping for school clothes, unencumbered by mothers, were two of my daughter's seventh-grade classmates, Lisa and Marcie. Lisa placed on the counter near the cash register one pair of pink Gloria Vanderbilt wide wales, one pink Gloria Vanderbilt V-neck, and a little print turtleneck—white with tiny red hearts—that I gathered was to go under the V-neck. I was impressed. All my life I have been trying to figure out how to put the right turtleneck with the right V-neck and here this child had it licked before she was old enough for a training bra.

"Well," said Lisa to Marcie, "at least you have one nice outfit." Clearly the Diana Vreeland of her generation.

Marcie took out a charge card and handed it to the saleswoman. "I hope you don't mind my asking," I said tentatively, thinking of the convenience of sending my daughter to buy her own sweater, say, instead of trekking down there myself, "but how exactly do you get to use your mother's charge? Do you need a store pass or something?"

"Oh, no," said Marcie, who was signing the sales slip with all the aplomb of someone who has been shopping the Horchow Catalog since she was six. "I had to start out that way, but now I have my own card. See? It says 'C' for 'child,' " she said, pointing.

Aside from defining once and for all a jap as someone who has her own Bloomingdale's charge card and a personal shopper before she is twelve, this incident has profound ramifications for parents.

Consider Marcie, who at twelve can buy whatever she wants at Bloomingdale's. There probably will come a day, however—perhaps when she is in college—when Marcie will begin to resent her dependency on her parents. She then will get a job and with it her own Bloomingdale's charge account and also her own Bloomingdale's bills. When her Bloomingdale's habit becomes too serious to support on her own, she will acquire a husband. This will work nicely until Marcie resents her dependency on her husband and she will get a divorce. Although she may for a while have to quit Bloomingdale's cold-turkey, eventually Marcie, having forged ahead in her career, again will be able to buy whatever she wants at Bloomingdale's, only this time on her own.

VIS

Theorists of the Women's Movement would say that this is the point at which Marcie has achieved true liberation. But what if Marcie, correctly having decoded the message of feminism as economic security, has developed along the way a taste for tax-free municipals? The answer is clear: Marcie must become a rich man's plaything who is liberated enough to maintain her independence while having her Bloomingdale's bills paid for her.

Therefore, the best way to raise a daughter is not only to teach her how to cook, clean, and iron, and not only to debate regularly with her the game plan for her achieving the Presidency (West Point for college probably is the right first move), but also to teach her how to exit gracefully from a limousine and that a lady always orders from the middle of the menu.

If you have qualms about starting your daughter out with her own Bloomingdale's charge card, you will be happy to know that Brooks Brothers offers the same service to adolescents of the male persuasion, leaving only one question remaining: how to raise your male adolescent to be a rich woman's plaything.

Suddenly Next Summer

Show me an adolescent in the last few months of the school year—that is, from early October onward—and I will show you an adolescent who believes that, short of a six-figure recording contract, summer is the most life can hold. That is because your adolescent has the memory span of a fruit fly and has completely forgotten last summer.

There really are not many options. Camp is the obvious choice, providing as it does a vacation for the adolescent's parents and relief for the mother who does not have the personality of a cruise-ship social director.[1] Camps for adolescents differ from camps for small children; in social structure they are closer to anarchy than to a police state, and frequently they offer a single area of concentration: gymnastics, tennis, soccer, weight loss—this last most often attractive to female adolescents who cannot easily be seen when they are standing sideways and who tend to start conversations with " My thighs are fat." "Wilderness" camps may be useful for adolescents whose idea of roughing it is sleeping without a top sheet. Many camps can provide the adolescent with desirable skills for later life, or, as one Fairfield County father remarked to a neighbor, "There are very few things we can give our children. One of the things you can give

[1] Not all adolescents, however, are willing campers. Some were packed off too early. "No matter what I say," announced one seven-year-old to his parents, "no matter how much I beg, don't ever send me to camp again."

your son is a really good serve." Occasionally camps are guilty of something less than truth in advertising; those whose brochures use the word "creative" often supply campers with devices intended to subvert the inevitable results of the word's original usage.

You may be surprised to find that your adolescent has no wish to attend camp with its best friend. This is because most adolescents prefer to lead a double life during the summer, a phenomenon particularly common among those adolescents whose parents transport them each year to a Summer Place. Like an accountant at Club Med, the adolescent unbends. Nobody here knows that it flunked Geometry, or for that matter got an A; nobody knows that of sixteen candidates for president of Student Council it received the fewest votes, or for that matter won. Occasionally there are problems with this new incarnation, as when your adolescent develops a taste for blue-collar romance, but for the most part the adolescent is content to bask in the social security of a place that is large enough to support only one pack of adolescents or where nobody gets left out because everybody's parents know everybody else's parents. The adolescent and its friends spend many pleasant hours swimming, playing tennis, bicycle-riding, movie-going, dancing, and most of all discussing how bored they are.

Some adolescents, eager for independence or faced with a Tostitos habit they are finding difficult to support on their allowance, prefer to seek work.[2] Unparalleled as a source of cheap

[2] Ordinarily this is greeted with enthusiasm by parents, although I am reminded of my friend Pamela, whose son, a freshman at Harvard, called during his first term to report that he had earned thirty-five dollars the day before. "Good for you," said Pamela enthusiastically. "Doing what?" "Cleaning houses," said her son.

HI FI
HI FI

HI FI
IN
SOUND
HI FI

labor, adolescents lacking extensive criminal records often are sought after by summer employers. Unfortunately, such occupations as beach-chair transporter or test-tube centrifuger often do not comport with the adolescent's view of itself as a future captain of industry. What your adolescent feels it is best suited to is sitting with its feet on a desk in an air-conditioned office straightening out the company before it takes George and Ringo to lunch to discuss the new ad campaign. Chrysler never would have needed to be bailed out, your adolescent knows, if it had spent its summers working there.

Many adolescents spend at least part of the summer traveling. If you are affluent, you may want to consider a group tour for your child, although, especially on European tours where World War II surplus aircraft are favored, aphasia may be more important than affluence for a parent.[3]

Some parents prefer to accompany their adolescent on its travels. Now that the children are old enough to appreciate the experience and can drive for more than thirty miles without having to go to the bathroom, such parents see travel as an opportunity to educate and to raise aesthetic sensibilities in a setting where nobody has to take out the garbage. "Look," says the parent, driving through New England on a This Is Your Heritage Tour, "isn't that beautiful?"

"What?" says the adolescent, who has been reading *Rolling Stone* for the last fifty miles,[4] interrupting itself only to criticize its younger sibling's grammar, pronunciation, and height.

[3] "But when *will* the plane be here?" asked one mother whose daughter's flight was already three hours late. "Hey," said the tour director, "no problem. As soon as it gets in from Gatwick, it'll turn right around."

[4] Or *The Brothers Karamazov*. That's not the point.

"That mountain over there. That's Mount Washington, the highest point in New England. Also, a major Revolutionary War battle was fought in its foothills."

"Oh," says the adolescent. It glances up. "That's nice." It returns to The Clash.

"What's the point of taking you places if you don't even look?" asks the parent.

"*I* looked, Mommy," pipes up the younger sibling sweetly. "I think it's just beautiful, and I'm so happy you took us on this wonderful trip." Yes, there truly are times when you wish a policeman would stop you for speeding.

Show me an adolescent at the end of its summer vacation and I will show you an adolescent who believes that, short of a six-figure recording contract, the first day of school is the most life can hold.

CANCER

Sun (and Daughter) Signs

There are many problems with astrology, not the least of which is whether there's anything to it at all. I never thought there was until I went to work on a magazine where editing the horoscope column was among my tasks. When the first forecast for my sign came in at something less than rosy, I walked up to the horoscope columnist. "Well," I said, "we'll have no more of this! As long as I'm in charge I want all the Virgo forecasts to be wonderful. I may not have much power around here, but at least I can control my future."

"Oh, I can't do that," said the horoscope columnist. "It's really all controlled by the charts. And as a matter of fact, Virgos are in for a really rotten couple of years."

And so they were. In any case, even if you do believe in astrology, you probably have not considered the ways in which it might be adapted to provide a clearer understanding of your adolescent.

Leo (July 23–August 22)

Leos are excellent administrators, popular with their peers, and natural leaders. Sometimes, however, they tend toward arrogance and conceit. Thus, while your Leo adolescent may be satisfied with being student-body president or leader of its motorcycle gang, to be on the safe side, you should plan to buy it a South American banana republic. Napoleon, Mussolini, Haile Selassie, and Jacqueline Onassis were born under Leo.

VIRGO

Virgo (August 23–September 22)

The person born under the sign of Virgo is practical, meticulous, and perfectionistic. As a child, it never colors outside the lines. The Virgo adolescent keeps its room neat and spends much time recopying its homework; generally it regards its parents, even if they too are Virgos, as disorganized, irresponsible, and probably beyond redemption, although God knows that's not for its own lack of trying.

Libra (September 23–October 23)

A Libran's taste generally is impeccable and they love harmony and beauty, which means your Libran adolescent daughter not only may consent to watch the Miss America Pageant with you but even may show an interest in your stories of the Princesses Margaret Rose and Lilibet. If you are the parent of a Libran adolescent, however, your best bet probably is to diet yourself down to its size and treat it well, in which case it may lend you some of its clothes.

Scorpio (October 24–November 21)

The Scorpion is brave, courageous, strong-willed, and rarely frightened by obstacles. Take baskets of fruit to your friends who are parents of Scorpion adolescents. If you are yourself the parent of one, consider boarding school for your adolescent, or for yourself. Charles de Gaulle, Indira Gandhi, and Chiang Kai-shek were born under Scorpio. So was Tatum O'Neal. Next time get pregnant in a different month.

Sagittarius (November 22–December 21)

People born under this sign are honest and forthright, earnest and open; they do not believe in deceit or pretension and never call home long-distance person-to-person collect to themselves. The parent of an adolescent Sagittarian should be prepared to be

AQUARIUS

told in vivid detail all of his or her faults, often in the presence of others. Keep your tax return to yourself.

Capricorn (December 22–January 19)

The Capricorn is dependable, reliable, hard-working, and honest. However, Richard Nixon is a Capricorn, which seems to cast some doubt on this whole exercise. On the other hand, maybe Richard Nixon lied about when he was born. Capricorn adolescents are no trouble with haircuts but will never take you to a *Bow Wow Wow* concert.

Aquarius (January 20–February 18)

The Aquarian is the most tolerant of all the Zodiac personalities. What this means is that there will be some very strange people, and possibly some very strange substances, in your house, and your Aquarian adolescent's tolerance may stop short of you when you fail to appreciate that it is fifty years ahead of its time. Farrah Fawcett-Majors is an Aquarian, but then, so is Ronald Reagan.

Pisces (February 19–March 20)

On the one hand, Pisces are sympathetic, accepting, and intuitive. On the other hand, they often are moody and depressed and short on will power. If you had a Piscean adolescent around at the same time you had a Scorpion adolescent around, baskets of fruit definitely would not do it. Even boarding school might not do it. Getting yourself frozen until it all was over might possibly do it.

Aries (March 21–April 19)

People born under this sign often are strong and enthusiastic, with quick and active minds, the sort who walked early and climbed out of their cribs and stuck pointy things into electrical

outlets. Ariens also tend to be stubborn. If your adolescent is an Arien, whether or not you continue to keep your electrical outlets covered is up to you, but make sure you're in training before you threaten physical violence.

Taurus (April 20–May 20)

The person born under Taurus is characterized by his ability to concentrate and by his tenacity. Usually, however, the Taurean is cautious and weighs pros and cons before taking risks, which makes him a not ideal doubles partner. If your adolescent is a Taurean, begin to elicit its summer plans in early September; if it is getting on your nerves, send it someplace to decide whether it wants its room painted blue or green.

Gemini (May 21–June 21)

The Geminian is charming, a good conversationalist, and easy-going, all of which make the adolescent Gemini much sought after by its peers. By and large this is a good thing, since chronic depression is less prevalent among adolescents who are popular; occasionally, however, this poses a problem, especially for parents of female Geminians, especially the part about easy-going. Brooke Shields is a Gemini.

Cancer (June 22–July 22)

The person born under Cancer is understanding, loving, sympathetic, kind, tender, and giving. If that description does not seem to fit your Cancer adolescent's attitude toward you, note how it behaves toward its cat, its dog, its parakeet, the pigeons in the park. Cheer up, though. Cancer is the most maternal of signs, and the Cancer adolescent is therefore the most likely to have an adolescent of its own someday.

Nine to Five to Nine to Five to Nine

Every mother who works outside the home yearns for the day when her child will become someone who can be trusted to light an oven, someone who can stay home by itself with the sniffles, someone who not only doesn't mind if Mother is not there after school but would as soon Mother worked in Alaska. In short, an adolescent.

Consider the downside risk, however. For one thing, the adolescent of the working mother often accepts its new responsibilities with the zeal of a reformed chain smoker. Ask it to make a salad for dinner and it responds by reminding you that you still haven't written to Great Aunt Charlotte. Tell it it is old enough to defrost the refrigerator and it asks you where you were until two A.M. on Saturday night. "How many times must I tell you to turn off the air-conditioner when you leave in the morning?" the adolescent berates its mother as she staggers in after work. "You really ought to use coupons when you shop," it says as it whips out of the oven a batch of chocolate-chip cookies. Suggest to your adolescent that, considering how much your time is worth, it doesn't pay to clip coupons, in fact it is more economical to phone in an order to the local grocery, a branch of Tiffany's, and your adolescent will mutter under its breath about lack of responsibility and people who don't recap soda bottles.

Your adolescent is, moreover, far less easy to impress than your child was. The days are gone when desk calendars, plastic promotional items, and gaily decorated Christmas cards were greeted with glee, when you could elicit bliss by bringing your Dictaphone home. Granted it is nice that your meetings no longer are interrupted by hysterical phone calls announcing that the gerbil mommy just ate her babies, there is something deflating about being told that the high-school Junior Investors Club just dumped your company's stock.

Paramount to the degree of respect you will receive from your adolescent is the extent to which your position enhances its position. If you had the foresight to get a glamor job—i.e., anything that brings you into contact with rock stars, any profession about which there is or has been a hit television series—keeping you employed has some marginal value for your adolescent. Otherwise, make sure to describe your day in terms it will find appealing. "I'm home a little late because I had to meet with the president to help him straighten out the company" is not bad. "I'm home a little late because I had to meet with the president of the New York Stock Exchange to help him straighten out the market" is better. "I'm home a little late because I had to meet with the President to help him straighten out the economy" probably is what you should aim for.

Even then, however, your adolescent will not feel your job should take precedence over its own care and feeding. That is because it has been spoiled. In part, that is your fault. Merely getting through the day as the working mother of a small child requires a flair for logistics that, properly harnessed, could make Amtrak run on time. But who stops there? Those couturier Halloween costumes you whipped up on the New York–Washington shuttle will return to haunt you. One adolescent called its mother at her office and asked for the name of the bakery where she got those terrific chocolate lace cookies last year. "I can't remember," said the mother, who already had used up her full daily ration of brain cells.

"God, Mother," sighed the adolescent, "you're really a sad case."

"I'm sorry," apologized the mother. "I punched it in and nothing's coming up on the screen. The computer is down."

"God, Mother," sighed the adolescent, "you really must be getting senile."

All working mothers of adolescents look forward to the day when they will be working mothers of working young adults and can interrupt their children in the middle of a meeting to ask them what they had for lunch.

"Most Important to Remember Is That We Represent Goucher College on All Occasions"

Who can fail to thrill to the stirring social codes of yesteryear? Goucher girls (the college flowers were ragged robin and coreopsis, my Freshman Handbook, on the contents of which I had to pass a test before I could date, reminds me) were not permitted to wear sneakers, shorts, or slacks on the streets of Baltimore, or to smoke on same, or to stay overnight in a hotel or a fraternity house. We had to wear skirts to classes and to meals, except during finals week and on Wednesday and Saturday at breakfast and lunch. Men were permitted in the dormitory rooms (only local and married students were allowed to live off-campus) from two to four on Sunday afternoon, when closing the door to your room got you a "Tone" warning (three of them and you were campused), as did closing the door of one of the ground-floor Date Parlours. The morality of the Honor Code, which required us to report a fellow student for signing in a couple of minutes early (ten late minutes—they were cumulative—got you campused), was debated earnestly whenever we weren't playing Bridge or discussing whether it was okay to Do It if you were engaged—even those who had, one knew, Done It in hotel rooms and fraternity houses from Hanover, New Hampshire, to Charlottesville, Virginia.

Surely an antique social code can't work nowadays.[1] Or can it? The virtue of this code is that it presents a complex set of regulations, the circumventing of which will provide your adolescent with an excellent vehicle for feeling it has put one over on you. Systematically breaking every rule, however, requires an attention to detail that will keep your adolescent too busy to do Something Worse. I therefore take pleasure in presenting the 1958–59 Goucher College Social Regulations. Even if you don't think your adolescent will go for it, put on an old pair of dungarees and slip into a pair of loafers, fix yourself a glass of whatever you drank twenty years ago, and enjoy the heady sense of nostalgia. If you are an adolescent reading this, here are the Olden Days, kid.

SOCIAL REGULATIONS

A written statement from parents or guardians concerning social privileges desired for the student should be filed in the Dean of Students' Office before permissions are requested.

In omitting a definite list of approved places, it is expected that each student will feel a personal responsibility in the choice of places which she patronizes.

A. *Freshman Privileges:*

I. General

a. The sign-out card is used when dating after 10:15 P.M. or when leaving the dormitory after 10:15 P.M.

b. Freshmen are not expected to date after 10:15 P.M. except on Friday, Saturday and Sunday for all three terms.

c. Types of sign outs:

[1] Here is what "nowadays" is: Recently I was at a party with a group of my high-school classmates. "Do you remember so-and-so?" someone asked. "You know, she had to get married." "God," I said, "do you remember 'had to get married'?"

1. 1:30 Saturday night with date.
2. 12:30 Friday and Saturday night.
3. 12:00 Sunday night.

d. Out-of-town and overnight permissions must be secured from the Director of the Dormitory or the Dean of Students, and students must sign out.

II. First two weeks: out-of-town permission and dating privilege is not granted until the student has passed her Social Regulations test which is given the second week.

III. First term

a. Friday, Saturday and Sunday nights are the only nights Freshmen are expected to be out of the dorms after 10:15 P.M.

b. Freshmen during the first term may have five 1:30's or five over-night absences from the dormitory, or a combination of the two. A Friday until Sunday absence counts as two over-nights.

IV. Second term: a maximum of four over-nights in Baltimore and an unlimited number of out-of-town permissions will be granted this term. A student may be away from the dormitory after 10:15 P.M. on Tuesday (without a date), and on Friday, Saturday and Sunday nights with or without a date.

V. Third term: Freshmen may be away from the dormitory after 10:15 P.M. on Tuesday nights plus one other week night (without a date) and on Friday, Saturday and Sunday nights with or without a date.

B. *Transfers:*

Transfers will be subject to Freshmen regulations during their first two weeks at Goucher.

C. *Sophomore Privileges:*

I. Sophomores are required to sign the sign-out card when leaving the dorm after 10:15 P.M. with or without a date.

II. After 10:15 date privileges will be granted on Friday,

IN
OUT

Saturday and Sunday nights and one other night per week.

D. *Upper Class Privileges:*
Upper-classmen must sign the sign-out card when leaving the dormitory after 10:15 P.M. with or without a date.

E. *City Over-night and Out-of-Town Permissions:*

I. City over-night permissions must be obtained from the Dean of Students or from the Director of the Dormitory. Permissions must be obtained before 10:15 P.M. Freshmen and Sophomores may obtain city over-night permissions on Friday and Saturday nights only. A student may stay two consecutive nights in private homes in Baltimore twice a term.

II. Permission to spend the night in a college dormitory other than the one in which the student resides must be obtained from the Director of the dormitory.

III. Any place beyond a 20-mile radius requires an out-of-town sign-out; any place beyond a 50-mile radius requires an out-of-town sign-out plus a permission which must be obtained from the Dean of Students or the Director of the Dormitory.

IV. All requests for Annapolis permissions must be filed with the Dean of Students not later than Monday of the week for which they are desired, so that the office may confirm reservations.

V. All requests for Y.W.C.A. over-night accommodations should be filed in the office of the Dean of Students. Any reservation not cancelled before 4 P.M. of the previous day must be paid for at the regular rate.

F. *One-thirty Sign-out:*
One-thirty sign-out privilege is extended only to students who are dating. There are no one-thirty sign-outs the Saturday before exams.

G. *Dance Regulations:*

I. When attending a Goucher dance a student must sign out and present her ticket at the door.

II. Students may not remain in the city over-night after dances given by organizations of the college.

H. Signing Out:

In order that students may be located in case of necessity, a complete sign-out must be made when using the sign-out card.

I. Evening Sign-out—

a. It is necessary for reasons of safety and convenience that the exact whereabouts of each student be known after 10:15 P.M. Students remaining out after 10:15 P.M. must sign their names and indicate their tentative destinations on their sign-out card. Students are not permitted to be absent from the halls later than 12:00 during the week and on Sunday. On Friday and Saturday they shall be permitted to stay out until 12:30. On Saturday night students with dates may remain out until 1:30 A.M.

b. All students with dates must sign the sign-out card after 10:15 P.M.

c. Don't forget that entertaining an escort after 10:15 P.M. in the dormitory is considered a date and you must sign out.

II. Absence over-night and out-of-town:

After receiving the proper permission, a student may sign out by signing her name, the name and address of her hostess, date, time of departure, return, and means of transportation. Whether returning from a date or an out-of-town absence, a student should observe her class permission privileges.

a. Going to one's home is considered as going out of town.

b. Dormitory students who go to the infirmary in Mary Fisher Hall must sign out to the infirmary.

I. Campuses:

A campus is conferred by hall presidents or Judicial Board upon violation of a college rule or regulation.

LATENESS OR CHANGE OF PERMISSION

Notification: If a student expects to be unable to fulfill the requirements of her permission she must notify the Director of the dormitory by calling VA. 5-3301, VA. 5-3302, or VA. 5-3303. The same applies if the student has failed to obtain her permission or to sign out before leaving. In this case, she should call, to get permission and to be signed out.

TIME ALLOWANCES TO THE CAMPUS

Downtown, Penn Station, Hopkins, Summit and vicinity, Strickler's, Four Corners, Greyhound Bus Station...... 45 min.
25th Street vicinity, Greenspring Inn and vicinity...... 30 min.
Friendship Airport (Baltimore)...................... 1½ hrs.
Trailways Bus Station............................... 1 hr.
Driving from Philadelphia........................... 3 hrs.
Driving from New York............................... 5 hrs.
Driving from Washington............................. 2 hrs.

DORMITORY OPEN HOUSE

A. Students may entertain guests and dates in their own rooms between 2:00 and 4:00 P.M. on Sunday afternoons.
B. Only invited guests may visit student rooms during open house.
C. Students are asked to sign their guests in and out of the dormitory. A guest card is provided.
D. There shall be no open house the weekend before examinations.

MAINTENANCE OF QUIET AND GOOD ORDER IN THE HALLS OF RESIDENCE

For mutual protection and to insure a regular time daily which can be devoted to study and rest, certain regulations are necessary.

A. Quiet Hours:

Comparative quiet in the halls shall be maintained in the afternoon.

The hours from 7:30 until 10:00 P.M. each evening except Friday and Saturday shall be observed as study hours, and strict quiet shall be maintained. Strict quiet shall be maintained in the halls after 10:30 P.M. every night.

B. *Smoking:*

1. No student shall smoke in college buildings except in specifically designated places.

2. The privilege of smoking in their rooms is granted to the students living in the dormitories. They are expected to provide themselves with ashtrays and metal waste paper baskets, and in case of damage to college property the individual student will be held responsible. They may not smoke at any time in the library, on the gym floor, or in the dining room or in Mary Fisher Drawing Room or Library except on special occasions.

SPECIAL REGULATIONS

1. Any student who marries during the college year must previously have notified the Dean of Students of her intention. Any student who marries during the summer vacation must notify the Dean of Students before returning for the fall term. Failure to do so makes the student ineligible to continue in Goucher College.
2. Regulations governing alcoholic beverages: under Maryland State Law, any individual under 21 drinking in any establishment authorizing the sale of alcoholic beverages is subject to fine or imprisonment. Students are reminded of the college policy which does not permit a student to keep or to consume alcoholic beverages in the college buildings. Returning to the dormitory in an intoxicated condition is a J.B. offense.
3. A combination of any three of the following will warrant an automatic campus: fire, tone, or quiet warning.
4. Students in groups of three or with escort are permitted to walk on the road to and from Towson after dark. Students may not accept rides from strangers. Such cases will be referred to J.B.

How Not to Embarrass Your Adolescent

Adolescence often can be diagnosed by inappropriateness of dress, inability to comprehend English, and a determination to turn the brain to jelly by bombarding it with raucous noises. One symptom, however, is incontrovertible proof the stage has arrived. Your adolescent believes, no, your adolescent *knows,* that every moment it is alive, the whole world is watching it, judging it, and pronouncing it gross. Except you, of course, but you don't count. In fact, you make things worse. If only they could, adolescents would lock their parents in closets for the duration. But, alas, your adolescent needs you—to drive it to school dances, for example, or to bear vast amounts of cash as it sets out on one of its outfitting expeditions. Following some simple rules, however, will ease your adolescent's burden.

How to Dress

Dress as though you were designed to go with the furniture or, better, to fade into the wallpaper. Maybe, your adolescent will think, with a little luck no one will notice you, or it, its devoutest wish. Women should wear gray, tan, beige, or navy. Avoid extremes of makeup or hair style; accessorize as though you were attending a funeral. Don't carry eye-catching items, like magazines; somebody might notice and be interested in you and, worse, speak to you. Parents of both sexes should have the decency to research beforehand school functions and vacation sites to find out what all the other parents will be wearing.

How to Behave in Public with Your Adolescent

The safest thing is to pretend you are traveling in a foreign country and have only a rudimentary grasp of the language. Do not speak unless it is absolutely necessary. Okay: telling the taxicab driver your destination; ordering food in the precise words of the menu. Use monosyllables whenever possible, and never draw attention to yourself by paying a compliment or making a complaint. A cold cup of coffee never killed anybody. Learn to read maps. Asking for directions shows how unbelievably stupid you are and makes your adolescent want to die, right there, in the middle of Tibet.

How to Talk to Your Friends in the Presence of Your Adolescent

Never discuss your adolescent when it is with you. That doesn't mean don't criticize it, which makes a certain amount of fragile sense. It means Don't Say Anything at All. Do not mention its tastes or proclivities. "Oh, Jerry likes the Yankees, too" is out of line. "Marilyn doesn't care for iced tea" will cause your adolescent to tell you afterward that it has never been so embarrassed in its life. Never breathe a word about your adolescent's good points, either. The same child who blushed prettily when you mentioned she had come in first in the fifth-grade spelling bee now will go into shock. It doesn't matter how high the honor. "Stacy has just won the Nobel Prize for Physics" is unacceptable.

How to Talk to Its Friends

Ordinarily this is not a problem, since your adolescent will spend every hour when it is not turning its brain to jelly devising stratagems to prevent you from ever coming in contact with its peers. When, however, that is unavoidable, never essay a conversational gambit. If you have known the friend for a long time—

since nursery school, say—it may be permissible to ask the friend how its parents are, or whether its pet dog is enjoying good health. But never solicit information or an opinion; don't ask what subjects it is studying, or whether it enjoyed the movie, dance, or date. Doing so will make your adolescent believe its friends think it has a nosy parent, requiring it to leave the States for several months.

How to Talk to People When Your Adolescent Is Not with You

Never volunteer information, especially to school personnel. "Jimmy is really enjoying math this year" or "Janet was pleased about getting a part in the school play" is the kind of breach of confidence that causes an adolescent to request a transfer to a good military academy. If you must tell your most intimate friends of kudos your adolescent has received, swear them to absolute secrecy. It could get back to your adolescent through one of its own friends, and then you will be guilty of having cruelly humiliated it by bragging. Parents who tell people whom their adolescent has a crush on should make sure their wills are in order.

Following these rules will not assure you of raising a paranoia-free adult, but it may cut down on your Valium consumption. And there may be hope. A fourteen-year-old of my acquaintance accompanied his mother and younger sister to the stationery store to buy school supplies. When he got home, he realized he had bought the wrong sort of filler paper.

"That's okay," his mother said. "I'll just take it back and exchange it."

"Oh, no, don't do that," responded the adolescent with horror. "They'll know I made a mistake and they'll think I'm stupid."

"Son," said the mother, "somewhere, deep down, you know that's crazy."

"Yes," said the adolescent. And smiled.

Carol Eisen Rinzler, formerly an editor and now an attorney, is the author of *Nobody Said You Had to Eat off the Floor* and *The Girl Who Got All the Breaks*. She lives with her daughter and son in New York City.

Devera Ehrenberg lives in Cambridge, Massachusetts, and her drawings appear frequently in *The New Yorker*.